To all the unnamed heroes of the Underground Railroad,
especially the thousands of enslaved African Americans
who risked everything for a chance at freedom.

And to the Africans who endured the harrowing
forced journey across the Atlantic. By choosing to survive,
they gave our nations the great gift of their descendants.

Contents

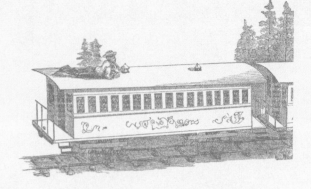

Acknowledgments

Most of the modern-day photographs in this book were made possible through the talents of photographer Tom Uhlman, who deserves special thanks. Thanks also to Robert Sexton for contributing photographs. Artist Megan Kelley has my deepest gratitude for creating and contributing a portrait of John P. Parker. Many thanks to Underground Railroad historian Henry Robert Burke for his inspiring research. Thanks also to Dave Uhlman for his expertise on Native Americans. And a very special thanks to Jerry Pohlen, a patient, attentive, and supportive editor.

Note to Readers

MANY SLAVES WHO ESCAPED had little or no help. In this book, the term "Underground Railroad" is used to describe the complete range of ways and means that slaves fled bondage.

Harriet Tubman's life story is featured in chronological installments at the beginning of each of this book's six chapters. While Tubman is perhaps the most famous member of what came to be known as the Underground Railroad, this amazing woman was only one of the hundreds of men and women who offered assistance, safe harbor, and guidance to runaways seeking freedom from slavery. Look for the "Hero of Freedom" heading throughout the book to learn about others.

Readers should be warned that some of the images and several of the directly quoted terms, phrases, and descriptions included in this book can be considered racially offensive by today's standards. These historical materials were left unchanged so that readers can experience for themselves the era they represent. Likewise, outdated, unusual, or phonetic spellings of quoted words have also been left unchanged. The dates stated in many of the stories and quoted slave narratives are best approximations.

The glossary on page 156 explains terms included in this book. There is a list of books to read, videos and DVDs to watch, and Web sites to explore starting on page 159. These will help you learn more about the Underground Railroad and discover places, possibly in or near your own hometown, to visit.

Time Line

STOWAGE OF THE BRITISH SLAVE SHIP 'BROOKES' UNDER THE
REGULATED SLAVE TRADE

Jamestown, Virginia, settled by English colonists — **1607**

Twenty captured Africans become indentured servants in Jamestown — **1619**

1640–1710

Slavery becomes a legal institution in British North American colonies

—

Africans and their children become lifelong slaves

Declaration of Independence proclaims "All men are created equal" — **1776**

1777–1804

Vermont, Pennsylvania, Massachusetts, New Hampshire, Connecticut, Rhode Island, New York, and New Jersey ban or phase out slavery

United States of America wins its independence, but slavery remains legal — **1783**

Northwest Ordinance bans slavery in territories that will become Ohio, Indiana, Illinois, Michigan, and Wisconsin — **1787**

New U.S. Constitution does not end slavery, as some had hoped — **1788**

U.S. population of 3.9 million includes 700,000 enslaved persons — **1790**

First fugitive slave law established. Slavery phased out in Canada — **1793**

Importation of slaves to the United States becomes illegal — 1808

1820 — Missouri Compromise admits Missouri as a slave state and Maine as a free state

Benjamin Lundy begins publishing the *Genius of Universal Emancipation* — 1821

1829 — *The Appeal,* by David Walker, urges slaves to revolt

First National Negro Convention — 1830

1830s — First uses of the term "Underground Railroad"

William Lloyd Garrison begins publishing *The Liberator* — 1831

Nat Turner Rebellion in Virginia

1833 — American Anti-slavery Society founded

Slavery banned in the British Empire — 1834

1842 — Dawn settlement founded

Frederick Douglass begins publishing the *North Star* — 1847

1849 — Harriet Tubman escapes slavery

Elgin settlement founded

Compromise of 1850 admits California as a free state and establishes a harsher fugitive slave law — 1850

1852 — *Uncle Tom's Cabin,* by Harriet Beecher Stowe, published

Kansas-Nebraska Act leads to "Bleeding Kansas" — 1854

1857 — U.S. Supreme Court's Dred Scott decision declares that blacks are not citizens

John Brown leads a failed raid on Harpers Ferry — 1859

1860 — U.S. population of 31.4 million includes 4 million enslaved persons

Civil War begins after southern states secede from the Union — 1861

Abraham Lincoln elected the sixteenth U.S. president

Emancipation Proclamation frees slaves in rebel states — 1863

Black soldiers allowed into the Union army

1864 — Congress rules that black soldiers must receive the same pay as white soldiers

Union wins the Civil War — 1865

1868 — Fourteenth Amendment grants African Americans U.S. citizenship

Abraham Lincoln assassinated

Thirteenth Amendment abolishes slavery

1870 — Fifteenth Amendment grants African American men voting rights

Preface

A Narrow Escape and a Secret Network

When Alfred Thornton first saw two men walking toward him one day in 1858, he wondered what they wanted. As they got nearer, Thornton recognized them as a local "constable," or lawman, and a slave trader. Now he was nervous. Alfred Thornton was a slave who'd lived on the Shinn plantation in Virginia all his 21 years. He knew that a slave trader coming for him meant only one thing—and it was about the worst thing that could happen to a slave. Thornton's master had sold him. That slave trader was coming to take young Thornton away, and the constable was there to make sure Thornton went without a fight.

Dread began to fill Thornton. Being sold meant he'd never see his mother, father, and friends ever again. He'd be moved to a new plantation far away. Thornton knew that the slave trader would take him into the Deep South. Everyone had heard how slaves were

ALFRED THORNTON BARELY ESCAPES CAPTURE BY A LAW-MAN AND A SLAVE TRADER IN 1858.

quickly worked to death on huge cotton plantations down there. The two men were coming closer.

In the instant before the lawman and the slave trader grabbed Thornton, the young slave took off. "I flew," Thornton said. "I took off my hat and run, took off my jacket and run harder, took off my vest and doubled my pace, the constable and the trader both on the chase hot foot. The trader fired two barrels of his revolver after me . . . but I never stopped running."

Thornton ran toward a pond. He jumped in and hid underwater. "I kept my head just above [water] and hid the rest part of my body for more than two hours." While hiding, Thornton thought about his next move. "I pretty soon made up my mind in the water to try and get to a free state, and go to Canada . . . but I didn't know which way to travel." Alfred Thornton planned on the North Star guiding him north. He tried to use the Big Dipper constellation to point out the North Star, like the old "Follow the Drinking Gourd" song explained. But a week of rainy weather hid the North Star behind clouds. Thornton spent night after night walking and wandering. He frequently lost his way, rested little, and ate even less.

But Alfred Thornton kept going. He finally managed to travel nearly 200 miles to the free state of Pennsylvania. Once in Philadelphia, he was helped by a group of people that secretly helped slaves escape. Thornton got on the Underground Railroad. It wasn't a real railroad, and it didn't run underground. But the name fit. Like anything underground, the Underground Railroad was mysterious and often difficult to find. Like a railroad, it quickly took people where they wanted to go. The Underground Railroad was a secret way that slaves used to escape. It was a loose network of people, pathways, and places that helped slaves reach freedom.

To help keep its people and places secret, travelers and workers along the Underground Railroad often spoke or wrote using code words copied from real train travel. Fugitive slaves were called "passengers," "travelers," "baggage," or "cargo." Underground Railroad "conductors" (like the famous Harriet Tubman) were people who worked in the Underground Railroad to guide runaways to freedom. People who mapped out "routes," "arranged passage," and made sure the way was safe were called Underground Railroad "agents." Safe houses, where runaways were sheltered, were called "stations." A person who ran a safe house was called a "stationmaster." "Brakemen" helped fugitives start new lives after they came to their final stops in free states or in Canada. The Underground Railroad helped thousands of runaway slaves like Alfred Thornton escape slavery. It was a one-way ticket to freedom. All aboard!

UNDERGROUND RAILROAD CONDUCTOR HARRIET TUBMAN.

Passengers

❧

Fleeing a Life of Bondage

HARRIET TUBMAN was born a slave around 1820 or 1821. Like most slaves, she didn't know her exact birthday. It's hard to keep track of dates when you can't read or write and don't have a calendar. Harriet's parents named their daughter Araminta. But by the time she was a teenager she was called Harriet. As a slave, she had to answer to whatever name her masters wanted. But Harriet said that when God spoke to her, he called her Araminta.

Harriet's family lived in one of the shabby slave cabins near the swamp on a plantation in the Eastern Maryland town of Bucktown. Harriet spent her first years barefoot and dressed in nothing more than a long shirt made of itchy cloth. When Harriet was about six, her master sent her to work for a woman who wanted a slave girl to babysit and do housework. Harriet was so young that she could barely pick up the baby. Harriet's new mistress, Miss Susan, was demanding and cruel. When the house wasn't cleaned to her liking, Miss Susan hit Harriet on the face and neck with a whip. Young Harriet had to sit up all night rocking the fussy baby's cradle while Miss Susan slept with a whip under her pillow.

Miss Susan eventually sent Harriet back to her owner, saying she wouldn't buy a slave

THE ARMS AND ANKLES OF SLAVES WERE BOUND WITH SHACKLES LIKE THESE.

so unfit for housework. So Harriet's owner hired her out to a string of harsh masters who put her to work running muskrat traps, cutting wood, and working in the fields. Harriet grew from a "difficult child" into a stocky, strong young woman known for her rebellious streak. Harriet's parents had been born into slavery, too. But Harriet's grandmother was born a free person in West Africa. She had been one of the millions of captured Africans shipped to America and sold into bondage. Perhaps Harriet remembered her ancestors' freedom, because she, too, yearned to be free.

Her rebelliousness nearly got her killed as a teenager. Harriet had tried to block an overseer, or slave boss, from chasing after a runaway. The furious overseer picked up a two-pound weight and hurled it at the fleeing slave. But the weight slammed into Harriet's forehead instead. It left her with a permanent head injury that caused sudden blackouts, or "sleeping spells," the rest of her life.

Harriet met and married John Tubman around 1845. He was a free black, and Harriet was permitted to live with him off the plantation. As a hired-out slave, she got around more than most slaves did. And Harriet was allowed to keep some of the money she earned. Her life was pretty good—for a slave. But Harriet knew the truth. She was

property. And her owner could sell her at any time to anyone. Two of her sisters had already been sold to a slave trader and taken away in chains, and Harriet had had nightmares ever since. She dreamed that horsemen came and dragged screaming women and children away from their families. The horsemen took the slaves away to a worse fate in the Deep South. Harriet Tubman refused to live that nightmare. Somehow, she was going to get free.

The Atlantic Slave Trade

Henry the Navigator was a Portuguese prince who'd heard from traders that West Africa was a land full of gold and treasures. The sailors he sent to explore the land in 1441 were the first Europeans to visit the western coast of Africa. (This was fifty years before Columbus sailed for America.) While the Portuguese sailors did find Africans who were willing to sell gold, the seamen soon found a different kind of wealth: slaves.

When the sailors arrived on Africa's western coast, they discovered that local kings ruled their lands with powerful armies and organized political systems. Slaves (mostly enslaved war captives) were one of the products sold in their trading networks. When the Portuguese arrived, West African rulers sold their slaves to the Europeans as well. In 1481 a West African ruler gave the Portuguese permission to build a trading outpost called Elmina Castle in what is today the country of Ghana. It was the first of many "slave factories" built by Europeans along the west coast of Africa. Hundreds of thousands of captured Africans were locked up in Elmina Castle. There they waited in misery to be put on Portuguese and Spanish (and, later, Dutch and English) ships. Their freedom was traded for gold, pottery, guns, knives, rum, and cloth.

The Portuguese and the Spanish began buying more and more African captives by the 1500s. Instead of taking them to Europe, however, the slave traders were instead hauling their human cargo to colonies in the New World. The business of shipping enslaved Africans across the Atlantic Ocean to the Americas came to be called the Atlantic Slave Trade. It was a dangerous, profitable, and devastating business that forever changed the world.

OLAUDAH EQUIANO
(C. 1745–1797)

OLAUDAH EQUIANO was born in what is today the northeastern part of the West African country of Nigeria. He belonged to the Ibo tribe and lived in a farming village with his family. At age 11 he was kidnapped and sold into slavery. He was sold from owner to owner in Africa, until eventually European slave traders purchased him and shipped him to the Americas. Equiano was enslaved in the Caribbean and later in Virginia. Then a British naval officer bought him and renamed him Gustavus Vassa. After 10 years of slavery, Equiano purchased his freedom with money he'd earned as a seaman. Once freed, Equiano lived a life at sea on expeditions and in naval battles. Upon returning to England he joined the British antislavery movement. He lectured about the cruelty of British slave owners in Jamaica and petitioned the Queen of England in 1788. At age 44, Equiano published his autobiography, *The Interesting Narrative of the Life of Olaudah Equiano, or Gustavus Vassa, the African*. It was one of the first works written in English by a former slave.

Vanishing Villages

The European slave traders and West African kings amassed huge fortunes through the fast-growing Atlantic Slave Trade of the 1600s and 1700s. Powerful West African "slave kingdoms" grew larger as they conquered their enemies with guns purchased with slave profits. Enslaved Africans were no longer only

PRINT ADINKRA CLOTH

MOST ENSLAVED AFRICANS in America came from West Africa. Many were Ashantis (ah-SHAHN-tees), people who lived in the area of Africa that is now known as Ghana. Adinkra (ah-DEEN-krah) cloth is a kind of hand-decorated fabric that is traditional to the Ashanti people. Adinkra cloth is covered with hand-stamped symbols. The stamps are carved from chunks of gourd. You can make an Adinkra-style bandana or T-shirt that celebrates the culture of the ancestors of American slaves.

YOU'LL NEED

- ⊠ Newspaper
- ⊠ Solid-colored T-shirt or bandana
- ⊠ Fabric pen or permanent marker
- ⊠ Ruler
- ⊠ Chunks of raw gourd, pumpkin, or potato
- ⊠ Small knife
- ⊠ Fabric paint of various colors
- ⊠ Dishes for paints

1. Spread some newspaper on a table. Lay out the shirt or bandana you're going to decorate.

2. Use the fabric pen and the ruler to draw a grid of lines on the cloth.

3. Make stamps by carving symbols out of the chunks of gourd with a knife. You can copy some of the symbols below, or invent your own.

4. Pour some of each color of fabric paint into a separate dish. (If they are too thick, follow the paint's instructions for thinning.)

5. Dip your stamps into the paints and stamp them onto the cloth inside the empty grid squares. (Helpful tip: Try your stamps on paper first to make sure you like the design and to get a feel for how much paint you should have on your stamp.)

6. Let your Adinkra cloth dry. Make sure to follow the fabric paint's instructions for washing the painted cloth.

being captured during wars. They were being rounded up solely for profit in slave raids. This devastated the lives of millions of West and Central Africans. The villagers lived in constant fear of being rounded up and captured by bands of armed men. Entire villages were wiped out by slave raids and wars of conquest.

One day, when all our people were gone out to their works as usual, and only I and my dear sister were left to mind the house, two men and a woman got over our walls, and in a moment seized us both, and, without giving us time to cry out, or make resistance, they stopped our mouths, and ran off with us into the nearest wood. Here they tied our hands, and continued to carry us as far as they could, till night came on, when we reached a small house, where the robbers halted for refreshment, and spent the night.

⊞ OLAUDAH EQUIANO, a West African, recounting his capture, at age 11, from the area now known as Nigeria in about 1756

The Voyage of No Return

Once kidnapped, a captured African's misery multiplied. Many Africans were taken from their homes far inland. The slave traders shackled these captives together and marched them toward the coast. Sometimes

CAPTURED AFRICAN VILLAGERS BEING SOLD INTO SLAVERY.

they marched many hundreds of miles in chains or shackles and were given little to eat. Disease and starvation killed many. Those who resisted were whipped or killed. Half of the captives died on these shackled marches, which were called "coffles."

Those captives who survived the coffles and made it to the coast were often locked up in the dungeons of slave trading posts, such as Elmina Castle. There they waited to be sold. Some might wait a year in one of the filthy, crowded,

ONE IN FIVE CAPTURED AFRICANS FORCED ONTO SLAVE SHIPS DIED ON THE WAY TO AMERICA.

dark dungeons. When a European ship arrived seeking slaves, the captives were marched in chains to the ship. These small sailing ships carried 200 to 300 human beings as cargo, as well as a crew. Most of the captives were chained together and stuffed into a hot, airless hold. Human beings were stacked on shelf-like bunks with ceilings so low that the captives could barely sit up or move. This was their home for the entire voyage. The so-called Middle Passage across the Atlantic took at least two months—sometimes four.

I continued to travel, sometimes by land, sometimes by water, through different countries and various nations, till, at the end of six or seven months after I had been kidnapped, I arrived at the sea coast . . . The first object which saluted my eyes when I arrived on the coast, was the sea, and a slave ship, which was then riding at anchor, and waiting for its cargo. These filled me with astonishment, which was soon converted into terror . . . I was now persuaded that I had gotten into a world of bad spirits, and that they were going to kill me. Their complexions, too, differing so much from ours, their long hair, and the language they spoke (which was very different from any I had ever heard), united to confirm me in this belief.

OLAUDAH EQUIANO, a West African, recounting boarding the slave ship at age 12, in about 1757

The journey across the Atlantic was horrifying for the captives. Aboard ship, the Africans were fed little and whipped frequently, and they were often forced to lie in urine, feces, and blood. It's no surprise that sickness and diseases were common. One in five captives died en route. Some slaves chose death over such a horrid life. There are tales of slaves jumping overboard or starving themselves to death. Some slaves were killed by their captors when they tried to resist or escape. The dead were simply unchained from the living and thrown overboard.

I now saw myself deprived of all chance of returning to my native country . . . I was soon put down under the decks, and there I received such a salutation in my nostrils as I had never experienced in my life: so that, with the loathsomeness of the stench, and crying together, I became so sick and low that I was not able to eat, nor had I the least desire to taste anything.

I now wished for the last friend, death, to relieve me; but soon, to my grief, two of the white men offered me eatables; and, on my refusing to eat, one of them held me fast by the hands, and laid me across, I think, the windlass, and tied my feet, while the other flogged me severely.

OLAUDAH EQUIANO, a West African, recounting his experience, at age 12, of the Middle Passage in about 1757

Those who chose to live and managed to survive the journey were sold into slavery in the Caribbean and the Americas. Many of the first slave ships that traveled to North American colonies landed in Virginia and Maryland, in port cities on the Chesapeake Bay. Later, southern port cities including Charleston, South Carolina; Savannah, Georgia; and New Orleans, Louisiana, became the favored places to sell slave cargo.

As arriving slave ships sailed into ports, news would spread of their arrival. Plantation owners and others seeking slaves soon made their way to the docks. Meanwhile, the slave ship's crew herded its human cargo out of the dark, smelly hold. Barefoot and half-naked, the Africans squinted in the sunlight and shivered in the cold. The captives were cleaned up and made to look as "high quality" as possible. The slave sellers tried to cover up gray hair, sores, and scars with paint. They forced their captives to sing, dance, and act happy and healthy in front of the customers. Slave buyers and plantation owners poked and prodded the human merchandise, checking their eyes and teeth as if they were livestock. Once the selling started, each African was sold to the highest bidder. Many slave buyers preferred to separate families and tribes. They figured that it'd be harder for slaves to escape if they knew no one and couldn't communicate with their loved ones.

Wives and husbands were separated. Brothers and sisters gazed at each other for the final time in their lives. If a buyer wanted a woman slave, but not her children, the children were sold to someone else. Whomever bought the slaves called them whatever they wanted, never even asking for their African names.

◈◈ *I was born at Edenton, [North Carolina,] on the sea shore, in 1804. It was an old shipping port, where a good deal of rice and cotton was taken away on ships and it was also a sort of slave market. Colored people were run over there from Africa and put into pens, and negro traders came there by the hundreds, bought the slaves and took them west and sold them to planters. When the traders and owners were making bargains they would feel you all over to see if your muscles were good, look at your teeth and ask what was your age. The buyer would ask what was your age and the seller would tell the year you was born. I was sold several times and that is the way I know I was born in 1804. I don't know the day or the month.*

▨ ALLEN SIDNEY, former North Carolina slave

The slave ships transported 10 million Africans to the Americas. It was the largest forced migration of people in world history. The Atlantic slave trade spawned shipbuilding and other industries in Europe. It fueled European

TO BE SOLD, on board the Ship *Bance-Island*, on tuesday the 6th of *May* next, at *Ashley-Ferry*; a choice cargo of about 250 fine healthy NEGROES, just arrived from the Windward & Rice Coast. —The utmost care has already been taken, and shall be continued, to keep them free from the least danger of being infected with the SMALL-POX, no boat having been on board, and all other communication with people from *Charles-Town* prevented.

Austin, Laurens, & Appleby.

N. B. Full one Half of the above Negroes have had the SMALL-POX in their own Country.

THIS 1780S NEWSPAPER ADVERTISEMENT ANNOUNCES A SLAVE SALE IN CHARLESTON, SOUTH CAROLINA.

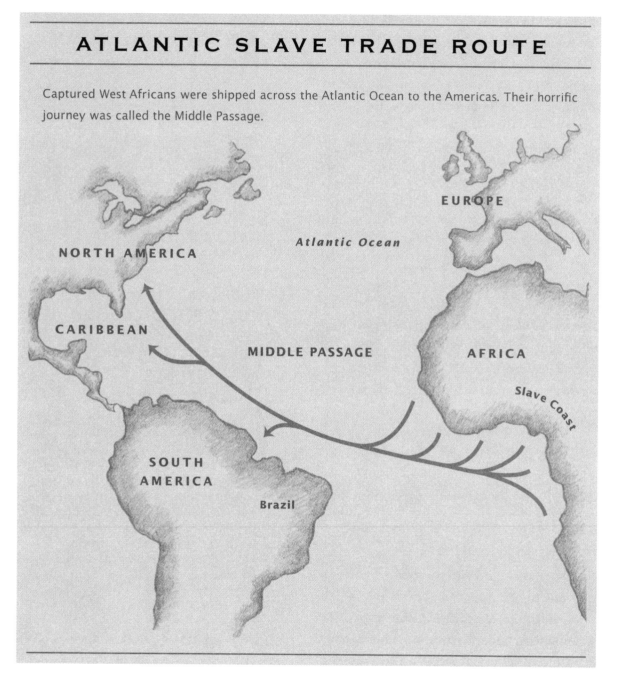

ATLANTIC SLAVE TRADE ROUTE

Captured West Africans were shipped across the Atlantic Ocean to the Americas. Their horrific journey was called the Middle Passage.

EUROPE

Atlantic Ocean

NORTH AMERICA

CARIBBEAN

MIDDLE PASSAGE

AFRICA

Slave Coast

SOUTH AMERICA

Brazil

colonial conquest and rule, and set England on the path to becoming the British Empire. The buying and selling of human beings had become part of the world's economy.

Slavery and Africans in America

Africans have played a part in the history of the United States since its beginning. African sailors, pirates, workers, and slaves came to the New World in the earliest European exploratory missions. The first enslaved Africans began arriving in the New World in 1518. They were brought to Europe's newly born Caribbean colonies. There they were put to work growing sugarcane and other crops for export, mining, and constructing a colonial empire that would soon wipe out most of the native Caribbean peoples. The great majority of the Africans sold into the Atlantic slave trade over the next three centuries would end up in the Caribbean and Brazil. About two-thirds of the approximately 10 million Africans shipped to the New World became slaves in sugarcane colonies. About a half-million slaves were brought to what became the United States. The first Africans arrived in Virginia in 1619.

The people of Jamestown, Virginia, noticed the newly arrived ship anchored at the mouth of the James River after the storm passed that day in 1619. But they took even more notice of what was aboard the anchored Dutch man-of-war. Twenty African captives were on the ship. The warship had pirated 100 Africans from the cargo of a Spanish frigate sailing the Atlantic Ocean. Eighty of the Africans had died at sea. The 20 survivors were the first Africans to arrive in what would someday become the United States. The Jamestown colonists traded the sailors food for the Africans, baptized them, and gave them Christian names. These first permanent North American residents from Africa—and other early African arrivals—weren't considered to be slaves. They were put to work as servants doing many of the same tasks as the English indentured-servant immigrants. The early Africans were likely free to go once they'd worked for 5 to 10 years, as was the case with English indentured servants. Some of those first Africans that arrived on the Dutch man-of-war probably became free blacks. Unfortunately, the African captives that soon followed wouldn't be so lucky. Within a few short decades, the Africans imported to the British North American colonies were declared slaves for life upon arrival.

Africans arrived in the North American colonies to find themselves isolated in a strange land. Often they were without any family members or even others of their own ethnic group

EUROPEAN COLONY	NUMBER OF ENSLAVED AFRICANS IMPORTED
Brazil (Portugal)	4,000,000
French Caribbean	1,600,000
Dutch Caribbean	500,000
English Caribbean	1,800,000
Spanish Caribbean, Central and South America	1,600,000
English North America	450,000

who spoke their language. Sold like cattle into a life completely controlled by strangers, they were expected to work for their owners for the rest of their lives. And their children born in this harsh land would inherit those lives of misery and pass them on to their own children and their children's children. Slavery had come to America—and settled in for a long stay.

Liberty and Justice for All?

In 1776 the 13 colonies declared their independence from Great Britain, and the American Revolutionary War began. In the Declaration of

RUN away last Friday Evening from the Subscriber, a Negro Fellow named **BAILEY** about 20 Years of Age, well made, about 5 Feet 6 Inches high, had on, when he went away, an old Bath Coat, and an Osnabrug Coat under it, an old Pair of short Linen Breeches, and an old Hat. He is supposed to be lurking in or about this City. Whoever takes up the said Negro, and brings him to me in Williamsburg, shall have a Reward of **FORTY SHILLINGS**.

—NICHOLAS SCOVEMONT.

FROM *THE VIRGINIA GAZETTE*, WILLIAMSBURG, VIRGINIA, SEPTEMBER 5, 1777.

Independence, Thomas Jefferson wrote: "We hold these truths to be self-evident, that all men are created equal, that they are endowed by their Creator with certain unalienable Rights, that among these are Life, Liberty and the pursuit of Happiness." But at the time, Jefferson himself controlled the "life and liberty" of more than 200 human beings—his slaves.

Just before the start of the American Revolution, nearly 400,000 slaves lived in the southern colonies, and 50,000 lived in the northern colonies. Why did the southern colonies have eight times as many slaves? Cash crops for export like tobacco, rice, and sugar grew well in the soil and climate of the southern colonies. Slave labor made large "plantations," or farming estates, profitable for southern planters. In some southern states, such as Virginia and South Carolina, the number of black slaves equaled that of white colonists. The weather and land of the northern colonies weren't suited for plantations, so fewer slaves were purchased to work in those colonies. In addition, a good number of the English settlers in New England and Pennsylvania didn't agree with slavery. Many religious settlers, such as the Quakers and the Puritans, had come to the colonies to build "utopias," or perfect societies. Slavery didn't fit in with their idea of a perfect society.

Many slaves escaped during the Revolutionary War. Some slave owners were Loyalists, who supported British rule. Others were Patriots, who fought for American independence from Great Britain. Many slaves took advantage of their owners' preoccupation with the war. They ran away and became free blacks. During the war, the British Army promised slaves of Patriot masters their freedom—if they fought on the Loyalist side. Some did, but thousands of others fought for America's freedom, even though the very people they fought to free enslaved them. It's estimated that 100,000 African Americans—most of them slaves—escaped or died during the American Revolution.

◈◈ *[P]eace was restored between America and Great Britain, which diffused universal joy among all parties, except us, who had escaped from slavery, and taken refuge in the English army; for a report prevailed at New-York, that all the slaves, in number 2000, were to be delivered up to their masters, altho' some of them had been three or four years among the English. This dreadful rumour filled us all with inexpressible anguish and terror, especially when we saw our old masters coming from Virginia, North-Carolina, and other parts, and seizing upon their slaves in the streets of New-York, or even dragging them out of their beds. Many of the slaves had very cruel masters, so that the thoughts of returning home with them embittered life to us.*

For some days we lost our appetite for food, and sleep departed from our eyes.

⊞ BOSTON KING, an escaped American slave who fought with the British during the Revolutionary War

Slavery Settles In Down South

After America won its independence in 1783, a group of men got together to write the U.S. Constitution. It was their job to decide what sort of nation the United States was to be—and to put those ideas in writing. Most of the writers of the U.S. Constitution believed that slavery would soon fade away. Many of the new nation's states took it upon themselves to "abolish," or end, slavery. By the time the U.S. Constitution was "ratified," or formally accepted, in 1788, slavery had already been abolished or gradually eliminated in Pennsylvania, Massachusetts, Maine, Vermont, Connecticut, Rhode Island, New York, and New Jersey. The Constitution declared that, 20 years from then (in 1808), the importation of slaves to the United States would no longer be allowed.

Much of the world was turning against slavery during the late 1700s and early 1800s. The governments of Britain, Canada, Mexico, and other countries were deciding that selling men,

HERO OF FREEDOM

BOSTON KING

(C. 1760–?)

BOSTON KING was born a slave near Charlestown, South Carolina. When he was 16 the Revolutionary War waged nearby. King decided to run away from his master and join up with the British army and earn his freedom. King served as a military messenger and an orderly. He survived smallpox and being kidnapped by a band of southern men who tried to sell him back into slavery. King escaped and rejoined the Loyalists who were fighting for Great Britain. After the British lost the war, Boston King and his wife, Violet, were among the 3,000 to 4,000 African Americans herded by the Loyalists onto ships in New York and transported to Nova Scotia, Jamaica, and Britain.

The Kings were taken to Nova Scotia, where the British settled them and other free blacks on rocky, barren land with few supplies. Many of these free blacks starved, but King got by, thanks to his skills as a carpenter. In 1792 the Kings, along with 1,200 other blacks, sailed for Sierra Leone, West Africa. Violet King contracted malaria, a tropical disease spread by mosquitos, and died soon after they arrived. King became a preacher in Sierra Leone, and he later opened a school. He eventually traveled to England to go to teacher's college at Kingswood School. After returning to Africa, he wrote his historic memoir, one of the few by black Loyalists.

women, and children like livestock was wrong. But slavery was growing even stronger in the Southern United States. Wealthy Southern plantation owners had power—and they had representatives in Congress. These representatives were able to add a number of laws to the new U.S. Constitution that protected slavery.

One such law said that persons "held to Service or Labour in one State" who escaped into another state "shall be delivered up on Claim of the Party to whom such Service or Labour may be due." This meant that runaway slaves were supposed to be returned to their masters—even if the runaway now lived in a free state.

Some laws protected slavery and others limited it, but no law shaped the future of Southern slavery as a much as the invention of one simple machine—the cotton gin.

King Cotton

Eli Whitney (1765–1825) needed a job after he graduated from Yale University. He headed south and became a tutor to the children of wealthy plantation owners. While working on a Georgia plantation that grew cotton, Whitney found his true calling as an inventor.

The small and bushy cotton plant grows pods full of seeds and fluffy fiber. This fiber is harvested, spun into yarn, and woven into cotton cloth to make many different things, including blue jeans and T-shirts. It takes a lot of work and time to separate the seeds from the cotton fiber by hand. One worker could spend an entire day hand-combing out the seeds from a single pound of cotton. Whitney invented a mechanical device that separates the seeds from the cot-

ton fiber. He called it the cotton engine, or cotton gin. A person operating the machine could clean 50 pounds of cotton a day, and a cotton gin powered by a waterwheel could process 1,000 pounds of cotton a day! Cotton exports jumped from 150,000 pounds in 1792 to 1.5 million pounds within two years of the cotton gin's invention in 1793. Northern towns quickly built mills to weave profitable cotton cloth.

The cotton gin created a great demand for more slaves, who were needed to work the fields and grow the newly profitable plant. Slave numbers soared in the south. The U.S. census counted around 700,000 slaves in 1790. Twenty years later, there would be 1.2 million slaves in the United States. Plantation owners frantically bought Africans who were shipped to America before the ban on the import of slaves took effect in 1808. They also purchased slaves from Northerners who sold their human property "down South" as one Northern state after

A MODERN REPLICA OF THE *AMISTAD* EDUCATES VISITORS ABOUT THE SLAVE TRADE.

SENGBE PIEH (JOSEPH CINQUE)

(C. 1811–?)

AND JOHN QUINCY ADAMS

(1767–1848)

IN JULY 1839 the Spanish ship *Amistad* sailed near the coast of Cuba. Onboard was Sengbe Pieh (c. 1811–?) and 52 other Mende Africans who had been captured in what is known today as Sierra Leone. They were about to be sold into slavery in Cuba. Perhaps meaning it as a cruel joke, the cook onboard the *Amistad* told Pieh that he and the other slaves would soon be killed and eaten. The slaves decided that they had nothing to lose by trying to escape. Pieh used a nail he found to unlock everyone's iron collars. The slaves found sugarcane-cutting machetes and used them to kill the cook and the captain and demand that the remaining crew take them home to Africa. But the *Amistad*'s crew tricked Pieh and the others. Although they sailed east toward Africa by day, at night they switched course and headed west. Little by little, the *Amistad* advanced toward the United States, not Africa.

After two months, the schooner landed near Long Island, New York. The U.S. Navy seized the ship, and the Africans were charged with murder and taken to jail in Connecticut. In 1839 slavery was illegal in Connecticut. By then it was also illegal to import slaves from Africa to any part of the United States or Cuba. (It was still often done illegally, however.) President Martin Van Buren (1782–1862) wanted the ship and its human cargo returned to Cuba. Others felt that, because it was illegal to import Africans, the men should be freed. The court case went all the way to the Supreme Court. Former President John Quincy Adams (1767–1848) defended the *Amistad* rebels. Adams, who opposed slavery, argued that the Africans had been kidnapped and were only defending themselves. He told the court that every person has the right to freedom. The Africans were found not guilty of murder and mutiny, and they were set free. Pieh and the others eventually returned to Sierra Leone.

SENGBE PIEH WAS CALLED JOSEPH CINQUE BY HIS CUBAN CAPTORS.

◈◈ *Dear Friend Mr. Adams,*

I want to write a letter to you because you love Mendi people and you talk to the great court. We want you to ask the court what we have done wrong. What for Americans keep us in prison. Some people say Mendi people dolt, because we no talk American language. Merica people no talk Mendi language; Merica people dolt! Dear friend Mr. Adams, you have children, you have friends, you love them, you feel very sorry if Mendi people come and carry them all to Africa. We feel bad for our friends, and our friends all feel bad for us. We want you to tell court that Mendi people no want to go back to Havana, we no want to be killed. All we want is make us free.

▦ KALE, an 11-year-old *Amistad* survivor from West Africa, writing in 1841

another outlawed slavery. No one in the Southern United States was talking about slavery fading away now. Luxurious lifestyles and plantation dynasties were being built on the bent backs of African American slaves. The slave population of the American South continued to grow, and by 1860 there were nearly four million slaves in the South. Slave populations grew fastest in the cotton plantation states, such as Alabama, Mississippi, and Arkansas. By 1860 slaves outnumbered free people in Mississippi and South Carolina.

We were now put to picking cotton. This is not so pleasant a job as might be imagined. The whole field is covered with "stinging worms," a species of caterpillar. At the setting of the sun each slave had to bring one hundred [pound] weight of cotton, which many of the weaker slaves could not do. In consequence of this, each night there were two hours' whipping at the "ginning house." . . . The cotton plant is planted in April or May, and the cotton is picked out of the pods in August. The heat of that month raises large bumps on the slaves backs; besides, the frequent infliction of the whip and the lash is almost intolerable.

JOHN ANDREW JACKSON, former South Carolina slave

SLAVES SURROUNDED BY THE COTTON THEY ARE PREPARING TO BE PROCESSED BY A COTTON GIN.

While nearly four million African Americans were enslaved in the United States in 1860, most Southerners didn't own slaves. Of those that did, about half owned fewer than five slaves. The majority of the South's slaves belonged to the elite, wealthy class of white plantation owners. Most of the country's slaves lived and worked on these big plantations with dozens of other slaves. By 1860, slavery had been a part of American life for more than two centuries. It had grown and changed over time into a gruesome factory-like institution. Slavery supported massive, moneymaking plantations owned by an elite upper class. It was based on racism, justified by a belief in white superiority, and continued for profit. The forced labor of millions was managed through cruelty, abuse, and imposed ignorance.

America was becoming a nation divided between North and South. Half of the young country's states were "free states"; the other half were slave-owning states. It was a troublesome mix. Northerners worked on small farms, in factories, or in trades, and they saw little need for slavery. Wealthy Southerners depended on slave labor to make plantation farming profitable. They wouldn't give up their wealth and power easily—nor without a fight.

Work, Punishment, and Food

The Greek philosopher Aristotle wrote that a slave's life was about three things: work, punishment, and food. That was still true 2,000 years later in 19th-century America. A slave's owner, called "the master" or "the mistress," made all the decisions that controlled that slave's life. Because slaves were "owned" by someone else, they couldn't own anything themselves—everything a slave had belonged to

WHERE SLAVES LIVED

This map shows where enslaved African Americans lived in 1860 by county. At that time, most American slaves were the working property of cotton plantation owners.

Percent of slaves per total population by county

■ More than 50% ▩ 10–50% ☐ Less than 10%

the master or mistress. Slaves were dependent on their owners for food, clothes, and shelter. The owner decided where a slave could go, the work the slave had to do, what he or she ate and wore, what a slave could say, whether or not the slave would be sold off, what he or she was allowed to learn, and how a slave was punished. Slaves didn't control their own lives.

Slaves were bought as workers, and work they did. Most slaves in America worked on plantations that grew cash crops. During the 1600s and 1700s that meant rice, indigo, sugar, and tobacco plantations. Cotton plantations became the forced workplace of most slaves in the 1800s.

Most plantation slaves were field hands. They planted, hoed, picked, and harvested the crops all day, every day. On a small farm, the master and his family might work alongside their slaves. On large plantations, the master usually chose one or more male slaves to be "drivers." The slave driver's job was to keep the slaves in line and to organize their work. He usually got better meals or a nicer place to live, and the other slaves often resented him. Slave drivers worked directly under either the master or the master's overseer, depending on the plantation's size. Overseers weren't slaves; they were employees (or relatives) of the master. It was the overseer's responsibility to discipline slaves and to make sure that all the work got done.

"Well, boy," said the overseer . . . "You are to stay here and act as driver of the field hands . . . So you may as well submit to it at once . . . If you don't, why, I shall have to make you 'hug the widow there,'" pointing to a tree, to which I afterwards found the slaves were tied when they were whipped . . . And this was my condition! a driver set over more than one hundred and sixty of my kindred and friends, with orders to apply the whip unsparingly to every one, whether man or woman, who faltered in the task, or was care- less in the execution of it, myself subject at any moment to feel the accursed lash upon my own back, if feelings of humanity should perchance overcome the selfishness of misery, and induce me to spare and pity.

JAMES WILLIAMS, former slave and driver on an Alabama cotton plantation

MOST SLAVES WORKED ON VERY LARGE FARMS LIKE THIS RICE PLANTATION.

Men, women, and older children all worked as field hands. Older men were put to work gardening or caring for livestock. Older women cared for children, cooked, nursed, and sewed. Young children weeded and cleaned the yard. Some slaves on a plantation worked in the master's house. House slaves cooked and cleaned for the master. They served as nannies, butlers, and personal servants. House slaves often lived in part of the master's home. Some plantations were so large, they were like a small village. On these kinds of plantations, slaves might also work as skilled tradesmen. These valuable slaves were blacksmiths, carpenters, wheelwrights, coopers, bricklayers, candle makers, and stonemasons.

About 10 percent of the slaves in the United States worked in places other than plantations and farms. Some worked in their owners' shops or homes. Others were hired out by their masters to work for others as cooks, nannies, riverboat hands, and shoemakers. Many hired-out slaves worked in slave gangs cutting trees, mining coal, building roads and railroads, or quarrying stone. Even if a hired-out slave lived away from the owner, the master collected the slave's earnings for himself.

I played with the massa's children until I became seven or eight years old, then I had to go into the field with the other black folks and work hard all day from earliest dawn till late at night. We ate twice a day, that is, when we got up in the morning we were driven out into the fields and were called into breakfast at noon by the blast of an old tin horn. All we got to eat then was three corn cake dumplins and one plate of soup. No meat unless there happened to be a rotten piece in the smoke house. This would be given to us to make our soup. Why the dogs got better eating than we poor colored folks. We would go out into the fields again and work very hard until dark, when we were driven in by the crack of the overseer's lash and frequently that crack meant blood from some unfortunate creature's back, who, becoming weary had shown signs of faltering.

John Jackson, former South Carolina plantation slave

Plantation slaves lived in wooden huts or log cabins. They were given an allowance of food every day and clothing once or twice a year.

Some slaves ate well enough and stayed warm during the winter. But most did not. Plantation owners wanted to spend as little on their slaves as possible while getting the most work out of them. That way, the plantation would make more profit. Most slaves lived on cornmeal and some bacon, beans, or molasses. Men often received more food than women, and children ate part of their mother's share. Many slaves fished, hunted, or gardened to supplement their diets—if the master allowed it. Slaves often went hungry, and overseers usually had to keep food stores under lock and key.

Our houses were but log huts—the tops partly open—ground floor—rain would come through . . . every thing would be dirty and muddy . . . My bed and bedstead consisted of a board wide enough to sleep on—one end on a stool, the other placed near the fire. My pillow consisted of my jacket—my covering was whatever I could get. My bedtick was the board itself. I only remember having but one blanket from my owners up to the age of nineteen, when I ran away. Our allowance was given weekly—a peck of sifted corn meal, a dozen and a half herrings, two and a half pounds of pork. Some of the boys would eat this up in three days—then they had to steal.

[S]ometimes many had to cook at one fire, and before all could get to the fire to bake hoe cakes, the overseer's horn would sound . . . I never sat

down at a table to eat, except in harvest time, all the time I was a slave . . . In the summer we had one pair of linen trousers given us—nothing else; every fall, one pair of woollen pantaloons, one woollen jacket, and two cotton shirts.

▨ Francis Henderson, former Washington, D.C., slave

A slave caught stealing food or anything else was undoubtedly punished. Slaves were also punished for disobeying orders, not working hard or fast enough, leaving the plantation without permission, or any other act the master or overseer deemed deserving of punishment. Slaves were considered property, and few laws interfered with a master's treatment of his slaves. Even where laws existed, enforcement was rare. Slaves were routinely yelled at, given a few "cuts" with a stick or riding whip, and kicked. Some were punished by being shut up in grain storage bins or toolsheds. Others were forced to wear iron chains or headgear for weeks or even months—while still having to work. Punishment could be gruesomely cruel, and it included branding with a hot iron, ear

BELLS WERE SOMETIMES HUNG FROM THE ENDS OF THE LONG RODS OF A HEAVY IRON COLLAR, AS SHOWN HERE. THE BELLS MADE IT DIFFICULT FOR THE SLAVE TO RUN AWAY WITHOUT BEING HEARD.

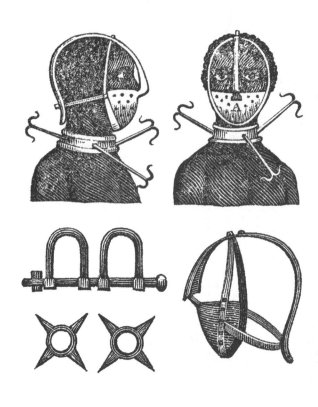

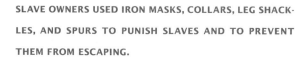

SLAVE OWNERS USED IRON MASKS, COLLARS, LEG SHACK-LES, AND SPURS TO PUNISH SLAVES AND TO PREVENT THEM FROM ESCAPING.

AS PROPERTY, SLAVES HAD FEW RIGHTS. SLAVE OWNERS WERE RARELY ARRESTED FOR THE MISTREATMENT—OR EVEN MURDER—OF THEIR OWN SLAVES.

My mother was a field hand, and one morning was ten or fifteen minutes behind the others in getting into the field. As soon as she reached the spot where they were at work, the overseer commenced whipping her. She cried, "Oh! pray" . . . I heard her voice, and knew it, and jumped out of my bunk, and went to the door. Though the field was some distance from the house, I could hear every crack of the whip, and every groan and cry of my poor mother. I remained at the door, not daring to venture any further. The cold chills ran over me, and I wept aloud . . . Experience has taught me that nothing can be more heart-rending than for one to see a dear and beloved mother or sister tortured, and to hear their cries, and not be able to render them assistance.

WILLIAM WELLS BROWN, former slave

clipping, tongue slitting, and even cutting off fingers. By far the most common punishment a slave received was a whipping. A moderate whipping was thirty-nine lashes on the bare back. Most plantation slaves—men and women—suffered through at least one severe whipping in their lifetimes.

Perhaps the worst punishment of all was being sold. "Troublemaking" slaves were often threatened with being sold or having their families sold away. But slaves were sold off for any number of reasons. Nearly every Southern town had slave traders who bought and sold slaves. A slave's price could be used to pay off an owner's debts after a poor harvest, or the money could be used to buy goods the master needed. Being sold was a constant fear of most slaves. A slave sold away would likely never see his or her family members again. Many slaves were sold at least once during their lifetimes. They knew what it was like to be taken from their mother as a child, or to have their husband taken away, never to return. And who knew what life would be like under a new master? Punishments might be crueler and the work even harder.

My brothers and sisters were bid off first, and one by one, while my mother, paralyzed by grief, held me by the hand. Her turn came, and she was bought by Isaac Riley . . . Then I was offered to the assembled purchasers. My mother, half distracted with the thought of parting forever from all her children, pushed through the crowd, while the bidding for me was going on, to the spot where Riley was standing. She fell at his feet, and clung to his knees, entreating him in tones that a mother only could command, to buy her baby as well as herself, and spare to her one, at least, of her little ones . . . [T]his man . . . was capable not merely of turning a deaf ear . . . but of disengaging himself from her with such violent blows and kicks . . . As she crawled away from the brutal man I heard her sob out, "Oh, Lord Jesus, how long, how long shall I suffer this way!" I must have been then between five and six years old. I seem to see and hear my poor weeping mother now.

JOSIAH HENSON, former slave

THIS 1860s STOREFRONT IN ATLANTA, GEORGIA, ADVERTISED "AUCTION & NEGRO SALES" AS ONE OF ITS SERVICES.

BUYERS CROWD AROUND SLAVES WHO ARE ABOUT TO BE AUCTIONED OFF.

Survival and Resistance

How did slaves survive the hard work, whippings, separations from family, and unhealthy living conditions? Many didn't. Illness, injury, and despair killed slaves every year. But those that did survive often relied on each other for comfort and support. Southern slaves formed communities with a culture that was rooted in their African heritage, but was unique to their lives of bondage in America.

Family was a big part of slave community life. Many slaves lived in extended families. Slave families willingly raised children who were left behind by parents who had died or been sold away—whether or not the children were actually related to them. No Southern state gave slaves the legal right to marriage, but many were married by local black preachers or in a simple ceremony called "Jumping the Broom." Most slave owners allowed their slaves to marry and have families for a number of reasons. Any children born to slave mothers were, by law, lifelong slaves and the property of the mother's master. This fact unfortunately encouraged many slave owners to impregnate their slaves themselves by force. Slave owners wanted as many slaves born on the plantation as possible, especially after the import of Africans to the United States was outlawed. Masters also felt that a family life tied slaves to the plantation. A slave with a wife and children was less likely to make trouble or run away. He'd be risking separation from his family.

❖❖ *[Our daughter] poor little Frances came creeping to her mother smiling, but with large tear drops standing in her dear little eyes, sobbing and trying to tell her mother that she had been abused . . . Her little face was bruised black with the whole print of [her mistress's] hand . . . Who can imagine what could be the feelings of a father and mother, when looking upon their infant child whipped and tortured with impunity, and they placed in a situation where they could afford it no protection . . . My happiness or pleasure was then all blasted; for it was sometimes a pleasure to be with my little family even in slavery. I loved them as my wife and child . . . but I could never look*

HOMEMADE HOECAKES

SLAVES WHO WORKED as field hands went to work early in the morning and didn't return to their cabins until late at night. The noontime meal, called dinner, was eaten in the fields. A staple dinner food was hoecake. Slaves took a sack with some cornmeal with them to the fields. A thick batter was made by mixing some water into the cornmeal. Then a slave would heat up his or her metal hoe by placing it in a fire. A handful of the cornmeal batter was baked on the hot blade. You can use this recipe to make hoecakes—without the hoe.

✂ *Adult supervision required*

YOU'LL NEED
⊠ 1 cup (170 grams) cornmeal
⊠ 2/3 cup (160 ml) water
⊠ 1/2 teaspoon (2.5 grams) salt
⊠ Mixing bowl
⊠ Spoon
⊠ Heavy skillet or griddle
⊠ About 1 tablespoon (15 ml) cooking oil
⊠ Spatula

1. Mix together the cornmeal, water, and salt in a bowl. Let batter sit for a few minutes.

2. Grease the skillet or griddle with cooking oil. Place the griddle on a burner and heat over medium-high heat.

3. Check the consistency of the batter. It should be coarse, with just enough water to keep the ingredients stuck together, but not be runny. Add more water or cornmeal if necessary.

4. Using the spoon, scoop out dollops of the batter onto the hot griddle. The batter will make two or three hoecakes. Once they are on the griddle, use the back of the spoon to pat each hoecake into a roundish cake that's about a half-inch (1 cm) thick.

5. Reduce the heat to low, and cook for about 5 minutes, until the hoecakes are brown on the bottom.

6. Use the spatula to turn the cakes over. Cook for about 5 minutes, until browned.

7. They're ready to eat!

STORY-TELLING GRIOTS

A GRIOT (GREE-OH) is an honored West African storyteller who is also the keeper of the tribe's history. The stories and poems that a griot tells are those of the tribe's battles and struggles; births and marriages; and poor harvests and times of plenty. West Africans brought their storytelling traditions with them to America when they were forced into slavery. It was illegal to teach slaves to read and write. Families depended on telling their history again and again for it to be remembered and passed on to the next generation. Stories that taught a lesson were also told, as a way for slave parents to teach their children values.

Turn your own family's history into a griot-style story. Or make up a story that teaches a lesson. Try to make the story fun and exciting! You want it to be a story that people will want to hear again and again. Once you've practiced your story, record it with a tape (or digital) recorder.

upon the dear child without being filled with sorrow and fearful apprehensions, of being separated by slaveholders, because she was a slave, regarded as property . . . She was the first and shall be the last slave that ever I will father, for chains and slavery on this earth.

⊞ HENRY BIBB, former Kentucky slave

It was illegal to educate slaves. A slave who could read and write and who knew about the world outside the plantation was more likely to resist or run off. But slaves told their children traditional stories and taught them how to cope with slavery. Slave children learned to speak their parents' language, a mix of English and African words that allowed Africans captured from different areas to communicate. Over time, this so-called Enslaved English evolved into a type of code whereby slaves could talk to each other without being understood by their masters. As the old saying goes, "Got one mind for the white folk to see, another for what I know is me."

Religion was a great source of strength for many slaves. The first enslaved Africans kept their native religious beliefs. But American-born slaves soon mixed their African spiritual beliefs with the new emotional, evangelical style of Christianity that became popular in the 1700s. They would gather at night in "brush arbors." Out of sight of masters and overseers, slaves sang, danced, and clapped to the preaching of black ministers. They played music with African-rooted instruments they'd crafted. These gatherings were a place outside of slavery. A place where African Americans could safely be themselves.

⧓ *Same time Marse John buy mammy an' us boys, he buy a black man name Joe. He a preacher an' de marster let de slaves buil' a bresh arbor in de pecan grove over in de big pastur', an' when de wedder warn't too cold all de slaves was 'lowed to meet dar on Sunday fo' preachin'. Yassuh, ole Joe do purty good. I speck he had mo' 'ligion dan some of de hifalutin' niggers 'tendin' to preach nowadays.*

⊞ WALTER CALLOWAY, former Alabama slave

African Americans enslaved in the South didn't like working for their masters any more than you would. Most resisted their owners as best they could without risking too severe a punishment. Slow or poor work and destroyed property were very common on plantations. Barns "accidentally" burned down, cotton was left in the field, tools broke, and horses mysteriously busted their fences and ran off. Groups of slaves often tried to work at the same slow-as-possible pace to keep any one person from drawing the wrath of the overseer. If a slave's cotton sack wasn't full and heavy enough at the end of the day, stones might be slipped in to trick the overseer. Slaves could also slow down work on a plantation by pretending to be sick or lame.

Not all slaves lived the same way. But if you were a typical slave during Harriet Tubman's time, you were likely born to slave parents who had also been born in America. You lived on a large plantation with many other slaves. Your day began before sunrise and was spent doing backbreaking work in the cotton, tobacco, or rice fields. You were given food and clothes, but owned nothing yourself. You'd been working in the fields since age six, and you were forbidden from learning to read or write. You seldom had enough to eat, and you had never seen a doctor. On occasion, you had been whipped for not picking enough cotton. When you were a small child your mother had been sold away, and you knew you could be sold away from your brothers and sisters at any time. You knew that if you had children one day, they, too, would be slaves. Perhaps, like Harriet Tubman, you dreamed of escape. But where would you go? You'd never been to school or even off the plantation. What was the world like beyond the fields of cotton and the rows of slave huts? Where was freedom? And how could you get there?

THIS FAMILY OF SLAVES INCLUDES FIVE GENERATIONS THAT WERE BORN ON A SOUTH CAROLINA PLANTATION.

RUBBER BAND BANJO

THE BANJO is an American instrument with African roots. Captured Africans sold into slavery crafted some of the earliest banjos found in America from gourds, wood, and tanned skins. They made the strings from a plant fiber called hemp or from animal intestines. Slaves' early banjo designs were based on instruments they'd known in Africa, and they called them "banjars," "bangies," or "banzas." As generations of American-born slaves built and played banjos, the instrument became popular with both black and white rural people. Today, modern banjos are used to play many kinds of traditional music, including jazz, folk, and bluegrass.

YOU'LL NEED

- ⊠ Plastic container about 5–6 inches (13–15 cm) in diameter and 3–4 inches (8–10 cm) tall, such as an empty ice cream or deli container, with lid
- ⊠ Wood yardstick cut to 24 inches (61 cm) in length
- ⊠ Pen that writes on plastic
- ⊠ Scissors
- ⊠ Business card or 3½-inch by 2-inch (9-cm by 5-cm) rectangle of poster board
- ⊠ Strong glue or packing tape
- ⊠ Ruler
- ⊠ Two 7-inch (18-cm) rubber bands of different thicknesses

1. Take the lid off the plastic container. Lay the shortened yardstick on top of the container. Use the pen to mark where both edges of the yardstick touch each side of the container's rim.

2. Cut vertical slits where the four marks are. The slits need to be about ½-inch (1-cm) long and cut through the container's lip. Bend the flaps of cut plastic into the container, as shown.

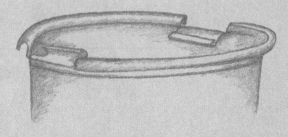

3. Fold the business card in half, then fold each end in toward the centerline, as shown below. Crease each fold well!

4. Fold the creased card into a triangular tube, as shown below. Glue or tape the overlapping ends together.

5. Set the triangular tube on its side so that the fold with no overlaps points upward. Carefully cut two tiny notches into this fold. The notches should be about ½-inch (1 cm) apart and in the center of the fold, as shown below.

6. Glue or tape the notched triangular tube onto the yardstick between its 1-inch and 2-inch marks, as shown above.

7. Place both of the rubber bands on the yardstick lengthwise, threading each through one of the notches on the triangular tube. Pluck them to check that they make different tones. If not, choose rubber bands that vary more in thickness.

8. Set the rubber band–strung yardstick into the slots cut out of the container. Place it so that the triangular tube sits just past one rim of the container.

9. Slip the lid of the container between the rubber band strings and the yardstick, and seal the lid onto the container.

10. Glue or tape the lid onto the container. The yardstick shouldn't move around. If it does, glue or tape the edges of the yardstick to the container. It's done!

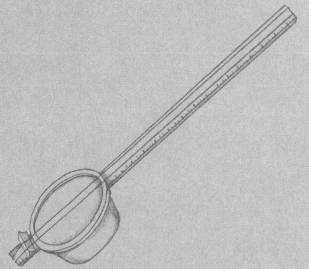

11. Play the banjo like you would a guitar, or African-style, by laying it on your lap. You can both pick and strum the strings. While plucking or strumming with one hand, use your other hand to press down on one or both of the strings at the neck to change the tone.

Ticket Agents and Railroad Operators

Fighting for Abolition and Aiding Runaways

HARRIET TUBMAN dreamed of escaping slavery. In her dreams, Harriet could see the green fields and welcoming people awaiting her across the line dividing slave and free states—but, try as she might, she never quite made it across to freedom before she woke up. "I always fell before I got to the line," she said. Harriet didn't want to be a slave. But if she ran away, would she really make it to the North? What if she had one of her sudden "sleeping spells"? If she were caught, her owner would likely sell her as punishment. She'd never see her husband and family again. Was it worth the risk?

Harriet made up her mind one day when she was in her late 20s. A slave from a neighboring plantation said that a Georgia slave trader was in town buying slaves to work on a Deep South plantation. Harriet was to be sold. The nightmare of horsemen and screams was coming true.

Harriet decided to escape. She couldn't tell her family. They'd be questioned when she was found missing, and she didn't want them to have to try to lie for her. She also thought that they might try to talk her out of it. But Harriet didn't want her family to worry about where she was, or whether she'd been sold. So she walked up to her owner's house and sang, "I'll meet you in the mornin', safe in the promised land, on the other side of Jordan, bound for the promised land." Harriet hoped the house slaves would understand the message behind her song and let her family know that she had run away. It was the best she could do. Harriet had to go.

Harriet Tubman left the plantation that night. She skirted the fields and swamps alone. She knew to follow the Choptank River to the Chesapeake Bay, which would lead her on to Wilmington, Delaware. It was only a dozen miles (about 19 kilometers) from Wilmington to the free state of Pennsylvania. The North Star would help her know she was headed the right way.

Walking at night and hiding out during the day, Harriet made her way northward. She kept away from the roads, and she knew to travel in swamplands to cover her scent and tracks. Harriet was careful of the friends she made on her journey, and no one she approached betrayed her. Finally, Harriet realized she'd crossed into the free state of Pennsylvania. "I looked at my hands to see if I was the same person," Harriet said. "There was such a glory over everything; the sun came like gold through the trees, and over the fields, and I felt like I was in Heaven."

Harriet made her way to Philadelphia and found work. She was free, but she wasn't happy. "I had crossed the line. I was free," explained Harriet, "but there was no one to welcome me to the land of freedom. I was a stranger in a strange land; and my home, after all, was down in Maryland; because my father, my mother, my brothers, and sisters, and friends were there . . . and they should be free." Harriet saved her money, swallowed her loneliness, and vowed to go back to Maryland and bring her family to the North.

Freedom's Lure and Risk

Throughout history, enslaved people have always found ways to escape. Slaves in America were no different. Nearly 400-year-old Spanish records tell of eight enslaved African men fleeing their masters in what is today Florida. Like many early runaway American slaves, these Spanish-owned Africans sought safety with local Native Americans. The Spaniards recaptured some of the Africans, but a few remained free, and they married women of the Ais tribe.

Escaping wasn't easy. Kidnapped Africans who were brought to America didn't speak the language of their masters. Many did not even speak the same language as fellow captured Africans. The new slaves knew nothing about the unfamiliar place they'd landed. If they did manage to get away, which way should they head? What plants and animals could be eaten? Where would they be safe? The truth was that there were few safe places for any escaped slave. The skin color of African Americans marked them as property. Any African American who couldn't prove that he or she was a free black or on a master's errand was a suspected runaway.

Even after slavery was outlawed in Northern states, runaway slaves weren't necessarily safe there. Nonslave, or free, states didn't allow slavery. But fugitive slave laws made it perfectly legal for slave owners and slave catchers to cross into free states to take back their "stolen property." The law saw an escaped slave as a thief and a criminal. Fugitive slaves had stolen themselves from their masters! While Northern free states were not a true haven for fugitives, by 1793 Canada was. Slaves who reached Canada were truly free, and slave owners and hunters could not legally recapture them there. Many American soldiers fought in Canada in the War of 1812. When they returned home to the United States, they helped spread the word about Canada's protective laws.

Let a man escape, and have but a month's freedom, and he will feel the greatest animosity against slavery. I can't give slavery any name or description bad enough for it.

Patrick Smead, a former Georgia slave who escaped to Canada

Running away was difficult for slaves. It was also very risky. Many runaways were caught and returned to their masters. All slaves knew—and most had seen firsthand—what happened to these miserable men and women who were recaptured. Being whipped was the mildest punishment they could expect. Many were forced to wear hobbling iron chains, collars, or bells to make running away harder. Some had an ear or finger cut off. Some returned runaways were sold away into the Deep South, where escape was more difficult. Even worse, an owner might sell a recaptured runaway's wife or family as punishment. An overseer or master might even hang or lynch a runaway in front of the other slaves as a warning.

Runaway slaves risked not only their own lives, but also those of their families. Many plantation slaves knew little about the world beyond the cotton fields and slave shacks. What they did know was often wrong. Slave owners lied to slaves about life beyond the plantation to keep them from running away. They claimed

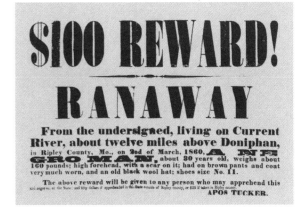

$100 REWARD!
— RANAWAY —
From the undersigned, living on Current River, about twelve miles above Doniphan, in Ripley County, Mo., on 2nd of March, 1860, A NE GRO MAN, about 30 years old, weighs about 160 pounds; high forehead, with a scar on it; had on brown pants and coat very much worn, and an old black wool hat; shoes size No. 11.
The above reward will be given to any person who may apprehend this said negro man, or the State; and fifty dollars if apprehended in the State outside of Ripley county, or $25 if taken in Ripley county.
APOS TUCKER.

that most free blacks were half-starved and that Canada was so cold that no crops would grow. Even if they managed to escape, where could they go? How would they find food and a place to live? How would they survive? What was freedom like? Escape was a difficult choice. Most slaves decided not to try to flee, choosing "the devil they knew" over the risks and the uncertainties of escape.

Slaves who were willing to risk escaping were often those who were in a better position than most to succeed, thanks to their particular circumstances. Thousands of slaves ran away during the Revolutionary War while their owners were away fighting. Many more slaves escaped from the Upper South, which was much closer to free states, than from the Deep South. Slaves who had worked or traveled off the plantation and knew the surrounding area were also more likely to escape. Lighter-skinned slaves were another group more likely to run away. If a slave could pass as a white person, he or she had a better chance of not getting caught.

Many slaves who decided to try to escape were those with less to lose. Slaves who were sold far away from their homes and families often ran away from their new masters. Slaves who discovered they were going to be sold and separated from their loved ones—as Harriet Tubman did—also often ran. As the former Delaware slave Jacob Blockson explained, "I made up my mind that I did not want to be sold like a horse." Better to run away than risk a new master.

Slaves also often ran away to escape whippings and other cruel punishments. Young women fled to avoid being raped and made pregnant by predatory overseers and masters. Women with small children to care for were less likely to risk escape than were single men. And young people were more likely to run away than the elderly. But mothers with babies, old men, slaves who'd never been beaten, and Deep South slaves are all among the escaped. Deciding to flee was something that every slave did for his or her own reasons. Those reasons were as varied as the people who acted on them.

❖❖ *No man can tell the intense agony which is felt by the slave, when wavering on the point of making his escape. All that he has is at stake; and even that which he has not, is at stake, also. The life which he has, may be lost, and the liberty which he seeks, may not be gained.*

▨ FREDERICK DOUGLASS, former slave and abolitionist

Fleeing Bondage

Henry Cox was a Virginia plantation owner who needed money to pay off debts. Cox decided to sell a young slave named Daniel Fisher. Fisher was taken from his brothers and sisters, put on the auction block in nearby Richmond, and sold to the highest bidder for $550. Daniel Fisher soon found himself in South Carolina and far from his family. After a few months, Fisher and another slave decided to steal a horse and run away.

In order not to tire the animal, we traveled from ten o'clock at night until daybreak the next morning when we ran the horse into the woods and left him, for we knew what would happen to us if two slaves were seen having a horse in their possession. We kept on our way on foot, hiding by day and walking by night. We were without knowledge of the country, and with nothing to guide us other than the north star, which was oftentimes obscured by clouds, we would unwittingly retrace our steps and find ourselves back at the starting point . . . One of the greatest obstacles we had to contend with was the crossing of rivers, as slaves were not allowed to cross bridges without a pass from their masters. For that reason, when we came to the Rappahannock [River] we had to wait our chance and steal a fisherman's boat in order to cross . . . While awaiting the opportunity to [stow away on a northbound vessel], we secured shovels and dug us three dens in different localities in the neighboring woods. In these dens we lived during the day, and foraged

RUNAWAY SLAVES TRAVELED BY ANY MEANS POSSIBLE—INCLUDING HORSEBACK.

for food in the night time, staying there for about three months.

⊞ DANIEL FISHER, a former slave who settled in Connecticut

Daniel Fisher's story has a lot in common with those of many runaway slaves. Most traveled at night—under the safety of darkness—and hid during the day. They escaped by any means available—on foot, on horseback, by boat, or by stowing away on ships and trains. Like Fisher, runaways used the North Star to guide them northward toward the free states and

MOST RUNAWAY SLAVES TRAVELED AT NIGHT AND HID DURING THE DAY.

took advantage of it. Some slaves simply fled their owners by moving into nearby woods and swamps. There they built crude homes or lived in caves. Groups of escaped slaves even formed a few "maroon colonies" in remote places, such as the Dismal Swamp, in Virginia and North Carolina, and the sea islands off South Carolina and Georgia.

Other escaped slaves were welcomed by Native American tribes, including the Ottawa and the Shinnecock. The Chippewa in Michigan, Ohio, and Canada took runaway slaves into their tribe, too. The Seminole tribe in Florida included perhaps a few hundred former slaves. The U.S. Army waged the devastating Seminole Wars in the early to mid-1800s in part because Seminole territory was a haven for runaway slaves.

Slave states and territories such as Mississippi, Alabama, Louisiana, Florida, and Texas were far from the North, and runaways had to travel many miles through slave state after slave state to get there. Some slaves escaping the Deep South headed for Mexico instead of the North. Mexico had granted freedom and equality to blacks in 1829. Some Deep South slaves escaped by boat to Caribbean islands. Others traveled by riverboat up the Mississippi River to free states. Slaves escaping from the Upper South near the East Coast stowed away on boats headed for Northern cities. Some even got on

Canada. Knowledge about the North and how to get there was learned from other slaves. Although it was illegal to teach a slave to read or write, slaves still passed information along in the form of songs, work chants, stories, and rumors. The journey north was long, and food was scarce. Runaways often spent all night walking and the day sleeping outside in all kinds of weather.

America had more wilderness during the time when slaves were escaping. And runaways

ships bound for England. Others headed north-ward out of slave states on foot, by horse, in wagons, or by train. Once in a free state, some settled there. Others moved on to Canada, either by crossing the Great Lakes or by travel-ing over land.

In the first place we took a small canoe and crossed the river till we came to a plantation owned by a man named Travis. He had a large sail boat that we desired to capture . . . We sailed all day and night Monday, and until Tuesday night about nine o'clock, when we landed just below Frenchtown, Maryland. We there hauled the boat up the best we could, and fastened her, then took our bundles and started on foot . . . How we ever passed through New Castle [Delaware] as we did, without being detected, is more than I can tell, for it was one of the worst slave towns in the country, and the law was such that no steamboat, or any-thing else, could take a colored person to Philadel-phia without first proving his or her freedom.

▨ JAMES LINDSEY SMITH, a former slave who escaped from Virginia in 1838 and settled in Connecticut

A Spreading "Sickness"

John Taylor and Monroe Evans were two Virginia slaves who were determined to

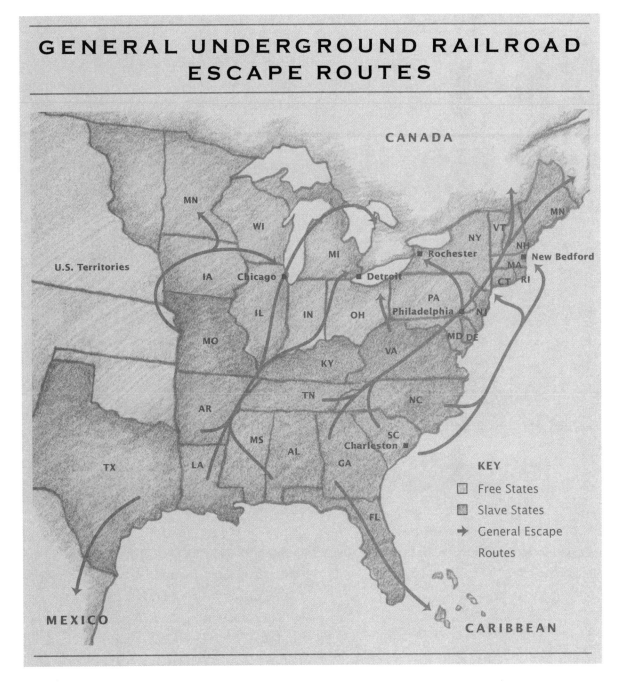

GENERAL UNDERGROUND RAILROAD ESCAPE ROUTES

CANADA

MN

WI

MI

NY

Rochester

New Bedford

VT

NH

MA

CT RI

U.S. Territories

IA

Chicago

Detroit

IL

IN

OH

PA

Philadelphia

NJ

MD DE

MO

KY

VA

AR

TN

NC

MS

AL

SC

Charleston

GA

TX

LA

FL

MEXICO

CARIBBEAN

KEY

☐ Free States

▨ Slave States

➤ General Escape Routes

SLAVE CATCHERS, BOUNTY HUNTERS, SLAVE PATROLLERS, AND JAILORS MADE MONEY CATCHING AND RETURNING RUNAWAYS.

escape. The overseer and his slave-hunting dogs caught them the first time they tried. Taylor and Evans were whipped until their backs bled, then washed with stinging saltwater. Four months later they tried again and made it as far as Tennessee before being caught. Another severe beating greeted them back on the plantation. Their master wanted to be sure his valuable property didn't flee a third time, so the overseer fitted Taylor and Evans with heavy iron collars. Three long iron rods stretched out from each collar and reached above the men's heads. At the end of each heavy iron rod was a bell. They were forced to wear the heavy collars 24 hours a day.

Wearing the huge, heavy collars, Taylor and Evans were put to work on the railroad and were watched all day. At night they were handcuffed and locked up in a pen for "troublemaking" slaves. After two months of enduring the pain of the collars, Taylor found a file in a tool chest. He snuck it into his pocket. That night, Taylor and Evans went to work escaping once more. Still handcuffed, they both lay down in their pen. Lying side by side, they were both able to tear off pieces of blanket with their teeth and stuff them into the bells. Now ringing bells wouldn't wake the overseer! Next, Evans got the file out of Taylor's pocket and cut off his friend's handcuffs. Taylor returned the favor, and the men went to work

cutting off the collars. Once free of iron, they climbed the walls of the pen and fled the plantation. The third time was the charm, because Taylor and Evans did eventually make it to Canada.

Taylor and Evans weren't the only slaves who were desperate to reach freedom. The Southern slave owners' "problem" of escaping slaves grew during the 1800s. It's estimated that as many as 50,000 slaves a year escaped. Many of these runaways were caught and returned, and almost every town in the South had slave patrols and special jails to hold captured runaways. Hunting down runaways became a business. All the newspapers were full of ads describing runaways and offering rewards for their return. People made their living breeding slave-hunting dogs or tracking down runaways. When the import of slaves became illegal in 1808, the price of slaves in America went up. Slave owners didn't want to lose their valuable human property. It was expensive to replace.

The "runaway problem" was causing trouble for the South in another way. Many supporters of slavery claimed that African Americans were content to be slaves—and that most were well treated. Many believed the idea that slaves belonged to an inferior race and needed to be civilized, Christianized, and cared for by owners. Besides, proslavery people argued, these slaves were born into bondage.

SILVER SEMINOLE GORGETS

ONE OF THE MANY Native American tribes that welcomed runaway slaves into their communities was the Seminole tribe of Florida. A few hundred former slaves escaped slavery by moving into Seminole territory in the late 1700s and early 1800s. The so-called "Black Seminoles" continued their African culture and often lived in their own separate villages. But they also intermarried and adopted many Seminole ways, including the Seminole language and style of dress. Like other 19th-century Seminoles, Black Seminoles wore turbans and adorned themselves with silver accessories.

They created silver armbands, wristbands, earbobs, headbands, and "gorgets" by heating and pounding silver coins. Gorgets are crescent-shaped plates, which were hung over the chest like miniature amor.

YOU'LL NEED
- ☒ Scissors
- ☒ Tape
- ☒ Disposable aluminum-foil cookie sheet
- ☒ Paper-hole punch
- ☒ Ballpoint pen
- ☒ 5-foot (1.5-meter) length of yarn or string

1. Photocopy or trace the three pattern pieces found on page 38.
2. Cut out the three pattern pieces and tape them to the cookie sheet.
3. Cut out all three pattern shapes from the foil. (Watch out for the foil's sharp edges.) These are your gorgets!
4. Use the hole punch to make two holes in each foil gorget. Use the paper patterns to guide you. Holes are needed in both ends of each crescent-shaped gorget.

5. Now you can decorate the gorgets. Use a ballpoint pen to "engrave" designs on the gorgets. Seminole silver gorgets didn't have a lot of decoration on them, but they did often have raised lines along their edges.

6. String the three gorgets together using the yarn or string. First, thread the smallest gorget with the string through its two punched holes, as shown.
7. Next, thread the medium-sized gorget onto the string. Tie knots where you want the gorget to stay.
8. Finally, thread the large gorget onto the string. Tie knots where you want it to stay.
9. Hang the strung gorgets around your neck so they lay on your chest. Tie the ends of the string together.

Continued on next page . . .

PATTERNS

SMALL GORGET

MEDIUM GORGET

LARGE GORGET

. . . continued from previous page

They knew no other life. How could they want to be free if they'd known nothing but slavery? But every slave who risked his or her life for freedom proved these ideas wrong. So did every former slave who lived happily as a free person in the North or in Canada.

They say that the negroes are very well contented in . . . slavery. . . . [S]uppose it were the fact the black man was contented . . . to see his wife sold on the auction-block or his daughter violated. . . . I say that is the heaviest condemnation of the institution, that slavery should blot out a man's manhood so as to make him contented to accept this degradation, and such an institution ought to be swept from the face of the earth.

J. SELLA MARTIN, a former slave and the first African American pastor of Boston's Tremont Temple

The argument over slavery was heating up in America. And fugitive slaves struggling for freedom made slaveholders look bad. Unbelievably, slavery supporters and slave owners blamed running away on a "mental illness" they called drapetomania. This claimed "disease of the mind" was named by the noted Louisiana surgeon and psychologist Dr. Samuel Cartwright. He prescribed severe whippings to cure and prevent "running away madness."

Standing Against Slavery

George Washington believed that slavery should be gradually ended in America. But he wasn't happy when his slaves ran off. In 1786 he complained in a letter that some people "would rather facilitate the escape of slaves than apprehend them when runaways." In another letter he wrote that one of his runaway slaves, who had fled from his Virginia plantation to Philadelphia, was helped by a "society of Quakers, formed for such purposes."

Most Americans had no strong feelings against slavery until the 1800s. But there were those who had stood against the enslavement of human beings since the first Africans were brought to North America. As Washington hinted in his letters, many early antislavery believers were Quakers. Members of a group called the Religious Society of Friends, these people were called "Quakers" because they trembled, or quaked, during their religious meetings. Quakers were also known for their plain, dark clothing and their formal "thee" and "thou" way of speaking. The Quakers were not liked in England, and many moved to America in search of religious freedom. Quakers were against war, and they believed that all men and women were equal in the sight of God. During a 1688 Quaker meeting, members spoke out against slavery, saying, "To bring men hither, and rob or sell them against their will, we will stand against." By 1761 Quakers declared that no slave owner could remain in the Religious Society of Friends.

The beliefs of many early antislavery advocates and supporters were rooted in their religions. Many Methodists and Presbyterians were also against human bondage. A number of the Founding Fathers of the United States also disagreed with slavery. They felt that it went against the ideas in the Declaration of Independence, such as the right to "Life, Liberty and the pursuit of Happiness." Ben Franklin, Benjamin Rush, Thomas Paine, John Jay, and Alexander Hamilton joined the antislavery efforts of Quakers and other religious groups. Rush, a signer of the Declaration of Independence, wrote in 1773: "Ye men of sense and virtue, ye advocates for American liberty, rouse up and espouse the cause of humanity and general liberty . . . Slavery is an hydra [monster-like] sin and it includes in it every violation of the . . . law and the gospel."

From Antislavery to Abolitionism

As the new nineteenth century dawned, more of the world was turning against the slave trade and slavery. Many who had come

to believe that slavery was wrong—including George Washington and Thomas Jefferson—thought that the practice should be phased out over time. While these people had some antislavery beliefs, they were not necessarily abolitionists. Abolitionists believed that slavery should be immediately abolished, or ended.

On October 1, 1835, abolitionist William Lloyd Garrison was warned that there might be trouble at that night's abolitionist meeting in Boston. Many Bostonians made their living manufacturing cloth, and they supported slavery because it kept the price of cotton low. When Garrison arrived at the meeting an angry mob forced it to stop, and Garrison slipped away to his office. The mob soon crashed in, but Garrison managed to escape through a window. Friends tried to hide him in a lumber pile, but the proslavery mob spotted him. The mob tied a rope around Garrison and dragged him through the street, tearing his clothes and calling for him to be lynched. Luckily, two men rescued Garrison and took him to the mayor, who jailed him for his own safety.

Garrison wasn't easily intimidated. Afterward, he even made fun of his attackers. Garrison was not afraid to say—or write—what he thought. In 1831 he published the first issue of his abolitionist newspaper, *The Liberator*, in which he declared: "Let southern oppressors tremble—let their secret abettors tremble—let their northern apologists tremble—let all the enemies of the persecuted blacks tremble." *The Liberator* published reports of slave abuse and successful slave escapes. He didn't care if his newspaper made some people angry; Garrison wanted slavery to end immediately.

❖ *Assenting to the "self-evident truth" maintained in the American Declaration of Independence, "that all men are created equal, and endowed by their Creator with certain inalienable rights—among which are life, liberty and the pursuit of happiness," I shall strenuously contend for the immediate enfranchisement of our slave population. . . . I will be as harsh as truth, and as uncompromising as justice. On this subject, I do not wish to think, or speak, or write, with moderation. . . . I am in earnest—I will not equivocate—I will not excuse—I will not retreat a single inch—AND I WILL BE HEARD.*

▣ William Lloyd Garrison, abolitionist and editor of *The Liberator*

Abolitionism Grows

The *Liberator* was seen as radical when it was first published. But more Americans

---

HERO OF FREEDOM
—— WILLIAM LLOYD GARRISON ——
(1805–1879)

WILLIAM LLOYD GARRISON began his newspaper career at age 13, apprenticing for a newspaper editor in Massachusetts. As a young man he took a job with Benjamin Lundy's abolitionist newspaper, the *Genius of Universal Emancipation*. Lundy's newspaper was published in Baltimore, in the slave state of Maryland. Garrison had agreed with Lundy that slavery should be gradually eliminated in the United States. But while in Baltimore, Garrison witnessed slaves on auction blocks, tied to whipping posts, and in chains. Seeing the suffering of slaves firsthand changed Garrison's mind. He started to disagree with his mentor Lundy about gradual freedom for slaves. Garrison became convinced that slavery was corrupting the entire country after he was jailed for calling the owner of a slave ship a robber and a murderer.

Garrison soon returned to Boston, and in 1831 he began publishing his own, more radical, abolitionist newspaper. *The Liberator* called for the immediate emancipation of slaves and for equal rights for African Americans. *The Liberator* was an important abolitionist paper, especially to black abolitionists. African Americans bought 400 of the 450 subscriptions sold in the newspaper's first year. William Lloyd Garrison helped found the American Anti-Slavery Society in 1833, the largest abolitionist organization of its day. He became a leader in the fight to end slavery.

---

were coming to believe as William Lloyd Garrison did. Slavery had to end—now! In 1833 the American Anti-Slavery Society was founded. Within a half dozen years it had hundreds of local chapters and 250,000 members in the North. Why did people believe that slavery needed to end in America? Many, like Garrison and the Quakers, had religious reasons. They saw slavery a sin that went against God's law.

Others opposed slavery for humanitarian reasons. They thought slavery was wrong because it was cruel and inhumane. No one should profit from human suffering. Another moral argument of the abolitionists was that "cruelty bred cruelty." According to that argument, slave owners and overseers who regularly whipped, beat, and sold away children they'd fathered were more likely to brutalize free people as well. Slavery degraded all human life.

It seems to be a law of nature, that slavery is equally destructive to the master and the slave; for, whilst it stupifies the latter with fear, and reduces him below the condition of man, it brutalizes the former, by the practice of continual tyranny; and makes him the prey of all the vices which render human nature loathsome.

CHARLES BALL, a former slave in Maryland, North Carolina, and Georgia

A popular novel published in 1852 convinced many everyday Americans that slavery was wrong. *Uncle Tom's Cabin* was written by Harriet Beecher Stowe (see page 44). The dramatic tale of the adventures and tragedies of the Shelby family's slaves was a bestseller. Two million copies were sold in the first two years.

Stowe was an abolitionist, and she wanted to open America's eyes to the tragedy of slaves being sold from their families and to the cruelty of brutal slave masters. While the book is fiction, its characters were modeled after real people. Their sufferings and struggles made readers recognize them as individuals with feelings and dreams, not just as nameless slaves.

Many Americans wanted slavery to end for practical—not moral—reasons. Many poor Southern whites found work hard to come by where there was free slave labor. Many settlers of the western territories didn't want slavery for the same reason. These "Free Soilers" were small farmers who didn't want to compete with giant plantations run by slave labor. Northerners also resented the political power of wealthy slave-owning Southerners. The number of representatives that a state is allowed to have in the U.S. Congress is determined by the number of people living in that state. A clause called the Three-Fifths Clause allowed each slave to be counted as three-fifths of a free person for representation in the House of Representatives. This meant that regions with slaves had more representatives in Congress than nonslave regions. This greatly increased Southern political power in Congress, and it helped to ensure the election of a long line of proslavery presidents, including Andrew Jackson, in 1828, and Martin Van Buren, in 1836.

Getting the Word Out

Both individual women and women's groups were very active in the abolitionist movement. American women couldn't vote in the 1800s. But women abolitionists organized meetings with speakers, held fairs and concerts to raise money, and boycotted goods made with Southern slave labor. Abolitionist women such as Lucretia Mott, Elizabeth Cady Stanton, Sojourner Truth, and sisters Sarah and Angelina Emily Grimke became leaders of the movement. At the time, it was still considered improper and unladylike for women to speak out in public, and many male abolitionists felt that these women were "forgetting their place"! Many women abolitionists, including Elizabeth Cady Stanton, would continue to "forget their place" and go on to fight for the right of women to vote once slavery ended.

How long shall the fair daughters of Africa be compelled to bury their minds and talents beneath a load of iron pots and kettles? . . . The Americans have practiced nothing but head-work these 200 years, and we have done their drudgery. . . . [W]hy have not Africa's sons a right to feel the same? Are not their wives, their sons, and their daughters, as dear to them as those of the white man's? . . . Oh, America, America, foul and indelible is thy stain! Dark and dismal is the cloud that hangs over thee, for thy cruel wrongs and injuries to the fallen sons of Africa.

Maria Stewart, an abolitionist and the first female African American political speaker

Free blacks weren't allowed to vote during slavery times. In fact, the U.S. Supreme Court declared in 1857 that African Americans—whether free or enslaved—were not U.S. citizens. (See page 15.) Many states in both the North and the South had laws that prevented free blacks from owning property, going to court, or even moving to certain areas of the states. As free blacks joined the abolitionist movement, they demanded more than an end to slavery. They wanted equal rights for African Americans. While white abolitionists wanted slavery to end, many didn't accept African Americans as equals. One man whose example changed the minds of many whites was Frederick Douglass (see page 48).

Frederick Douglass became determined to learn to read and write as a young child. In 1825, when he was only eight, his owner sent him away from the plantation. Young Douglass was put to work as a house servant in Baltimore, Maryland. There he often heard his mistress reading the Bible aloud. When he asked her to teach him to read, she agreed to do so. But by the time Douglass learned the alphabet, his

HARRIET BEECHER STOWE'S *UNCLE TOM'S CABIN* SOLD TWO MILLION COPIES IN ITS FIRST TWO YEARS.

HARRIET BEECHER STOWE

(1811–1896)

AS A YOUNG WOMAN, Harriet Beecher Stowe worked as a teacher in New England. But when her father, who was a minister and an abolitionist, moved to the frontier town of Cincinnati, Ohio, in 1832, she went with him. Reverend Beecher's Cincinnati home became a meeting place for abolitionists, and it was probably also a station, or safe house, on the Underground Railroad. The slave state of Kentucky lay just across the Ohio River from Cincinnati, and Stowe saw the evils of slavery firsthand there, including slave auctions. She also interviewed former slaves in Ohio who had escaped along the Underground Railroad. Stowe visited the home of famous Underground Railroad worker Rev. John Rankin (page 69), in nearby Ripley, Ohio. She also met Levi and Catherine Coffin (page 102), two important people in the Underground Railroad who helped many former slaves escape to freedom in the North.

Harriet Beecher Stowe moved back to New England in 1850 with her husband, Calvin Stowe. It was there that she wrote her most famous book, *Uncle Tom's Cabin*. Many of the characters in *Uncle Tom's Cabin* are based on real-life individuals that Stowe met or was told about. The brutality and misery suffered by the slave characters in her story turned many Americans against slavery. When President Lincoln met her he said, "So you're the little lady who started this big war."

master found out about the lessons and forbade him to continue. But Douglass didn't give up. He bribed schoolboys to teach him, and he collected scraps of books that others threw away. Young Douglass had no paper, so he practiced his writing on fence posts, using charcoal.

By the time Douglass decided to escape, he had learned how to read and write, and he'd read books about human rights and history. He'd also studied newspaper articles about the antislavery movement. Douglass wanted freedom and equal rights not only for himself, but for all African Americans. After escaping in 1838, he became a famous lecturer on the antislavery circuit, and he started an antislavery newspaper called the *North Star*.

Rev. Jermain Wesley Loguen (see page 101) was another former slave who published a newspaper. Loguen's fame and his *Weekly Anglo-African* paper allowed his owner to track him down. In a letter, Loguen's former owner demanded that he send her the money he was worth as a slave! Otherwise, she said she'd sell him to someone who'd come get him.

❖ *You say you have offers to buy me, and that you shall sell me if I do not send your $1000, and in the same breath and almost in the same sentence, you say "You know we raised you as we did our own children." Woman, did you raise your* *own children for the market? Did you raise them for the whipping post? Did you raise them to be driven off, bound to a coffle in chains? . . . Shame on you! . . . Before God and high heaven, is there a law for one man which is not a law for every other man?*

⊠ JERMAIN WESLEY LOGUEN, an abolitionist and a former slave, in a letter to his former master, dated March 28, 1860

A great number of former slaves and free blacks became influential abolitionists. Many African American abolitionists who had escaped their bondage still had enslaved family members or friends. All knew firsthand the hardships and unfair treatment that every African American, free or slave, suffered. How could they not stand up for freedom? By the mid 1800s, abolitionism had become a wide tent. It included supporters from many different camps of thought—not all of whom were in agreement. Supporters had differing reasons for wanting slavery to end—but they all wanted it ended. And many were willing to work toward that goal. Abolitionists organized rallies, meetings, and public lectures. They invited the public to come and hear about the horrors of slavery—often firsthand from escaped slaves. Antislavery newspapers, books, pamphlets, and broadsheets were also made avail-

able as a way to "transform the conscious of every American." Abolitionists agitated state legislatures and the U.S. Congress by sending petitions against slavery.

The self-written life stories, or slave narratives, of former slaves such as Frederick Douglass became popular in the United States. Americans loved to read these tales of narrow escapes and danger, and the stories created support for abolitionism and the struggles of African Americans. Many abolitionists—especially free blacks—worked to improve the lives of newly free slaves and other blacks living in the North. In a time when African Americans weren't welcome in most public institutions, they founded many schools and libraries for free blacks.

⊠ *I was born in Lexington, Ky. The man who stole me as soon as I was born, recorded the births of all the infants which he claimed to be born his property, in a book which he kept for that purpose . . . My master owned about forty slaves, twenty-five of whom were field hands . . . He had a large farm, the principal productions of which were tobacco and hemp. The slave cabins were situated on the back part of the farm, with the house of the overseer, whose name was Grove Cook, in their midst. He had the entire charge of the farm, and having no family, was allowed a woman to*

ANTISLAVERY HANDBILL

A HANDBILL is a single sheet of paper that is handed out in public places or delivered to homes or offices. Before the days of television, radio, or the Internet, handbills were commonly used to advertise products, services, and events, and to make public announcements. Antislavery supporters and abolitionists used handbills (see page 40) to announce antislavery meetings and to educate the public about enslaved African Americans.

YOU'LL NEED
⊠ Paper
⊠ Pen
⊠ Typewriter or word processor, if desired
⊠ Photocopy machine

1. Plan your handbill. What do you want to say and how do you want to say it? Do you want pictures on your handbill, or just words?
2. Lay out your handbill on a single sheet of paper. You can handwrite the text around pictures or use a typewriter or word processor.
3. "Print up" your handbills on a photocopy machine, then hand them out!

SOJOURNER TRUTH

(1797–1883)

ISABELLA BAUMFREE was born a slave in New York. All but one of her brothers and sisters were sold away from the family. Isabella, too, was sold as a child, once at age 9 and again at age 13. Just before New York completely abolished slavery in 1827, she ran away with her infant to the home of Quaker friends. They purchased Baumfree and helped her recover her other child, a small son who had been sold into slavery in the South. In 1829 Baumfree moved with her two children to New York City, where she earned money doing housework.

Isabella Baumfree claimed that God spoke to her in a vision in 1843. She soon took the name Sojourner Truth, and she left New York City. She chose the name, she said, "because I was to travel up and down the land; because I was to declare truth to the people." Sojourner lectured against slavery all over the United States. Her plain speech and strong presence made her a popular abolitionist speaker. Truth also spoke out strongly for women's rights.

Sojourner Truth collected supplies for black volunteer regiments during the Civil War, and she was received at the White House by President Abraham Lincoln. She later went to Washington, D.C., to help desegregate streetcars.

SOJOURNER TRUTH, C. 1864, AT APPROXIMATELY 67 YEARS OF AGE.

keep house for him, whose business it was to deal out the provisions for the hands.

☒ WILLIAM WELLS BROWN, an abolitionist, in his book, *Narrative of William W. Brown, an American Slave*

Protest and Colonization

Supporters of slavery didn't like abolitionists one bit. Angry plantation owners argued that fugitive slaves and radical Quakers had no right to take away their livelihood. Handing out, printing, or even owning antislavery literature was outlawed in much of the South. Many Southern post offices banned the mailing of abolition literature. They claimed it caused looting by slavery supporters who broke in to destroy the literature before it could be delivered.

Abolitionism was seen as a religious crusade to many Northerners. But many Southern clergy defended slavery as a "wise and beneficent institution." One minister reassured his congregation from the pulpit that "the institution of slavery was devised by God for the especial benefit of the coloured race." Ideas like these were based on the worn-out argument that African Americans needed to be cared for because they were inferior. Proslavery supporters played on Southerners' fears of having to live side by side with "inferior" African Americans if they were allowed to go free. In some parts of the South, slaves outnumbered whites. Some Southerners might have wanted to end slavery, but they didn't want to live as a white minority among free blacks.

The American Colonization Society's answer to this was to send freed blacks to Africa, beginning arouond 1822. Some free black leaders and abolitionists agreed with this idea because they believed that blacks would never be treated as equals in America. The society established the West African colony of Liberia as a place where freed blacks could emigrate, and thousands of free blacks did move to Liberia. But many more were against the idea. Most felt it was racist and unfair, and that white Americans simply wanted to get rid of free blacks but keep slavery legal. Many free blacks suspected that whites wanted them to emigrate so that they couldn't help slaves escape. But the main reason that most free blacks didn't move to Africa was because America was their home. They'd been born in United States, and they wanted to make it a better place for African Americans to live. Emigration to Liberia became another issue that abolitionists disagreed on, along with the role of women and free blacks in the movement. But some of the most heated arguments among all abolitionists were over slave rebellions.

Revolt!

Slave uprisings weren't unknown in America. Incidents of them were recorded as far back as the 1700s. Many slaveholders lived in fear of their slaves revolting. The masters knew they were outnumbered. But by the time slavery was confined to the South, slave owners had done a lot to prevent organized rebellions. Drums weren't allowed on plantations, because slaves could use them to communicate. Slaves often weren't allowed to travel, group together, have access to weapons, read, or write. Masters and overseers used whippings and other cruelty to punish any slave who resisted the master's will.

One day in February of 1831 a slave named Nat Turner (1800–1831) saw the sun turn dark in the middle of the day. Turner believed the solar eclipse was a sign from God, and he knew the time had come to rebel against his captivity. He and his followers, who were also slaves, began to plan a slave rebellion.

Nat Turner's mother had taught him to hate slavery early on. She was born in Africa and knew the pain of lost freedom. Turner learned to read from his master's son. He grew into a deeply religious man who had visions, saw miracles, and believed that God spoke to him. Turner soon became a well-known preacher in Virginia. In 1825 he had a vision where "white

$50 REWARD—Ran away from the subscriber, a negro fellow named Dick, about 21 or 22 years of age, dark mulatto, has many scars on his back from being whipped. The boy was purchased by me from Thomas L. Arnold, and absconded about the time the purchase was made.

—JAMES NOE

FROM THE *PORT GIBSON CORRESPONDENT*, PORT GIBSON, MISSISSIPPI, SEPT. 16, 1837.

FREDERICK DOUGLASS

(C. 1817–1895)

Born a slave in Maryland, Frederick Douglass knew the misery of slavery firsthand. Douglass wrote about how, at age six, he ate cornmeal mush from a trough with other slave children, "like so many pigs." Douglass escaped to the North by dressing as a sailor and boarding a train with fake "free black" papers. When Douglass heard the abolitionist William Lloyd Garrison speak in 1841, the former slave knew what his life's work must be.

Douglass quickly became a popular lecturer for the American Anti-Slavery Society. In 1845 he wrote *Narrative of the Life of Frederick Douglass, an American Slave.* The book was a bestseller, but his fame was dangerous—Douglass was still a fugitive slave. To avoid being recaptured, he spent two years lecturing in England. British friends collected enough money to purchase Douglass from his former owner, and the famous African American abolitionist returned to the United States a free man.

Douglass settled in Rochester, New York, in 1847 and began publishing the influential abolitionist newspaper the *North Star.* The Douglass family home was also an Underground Railroad station, and it sheltered dozens of runaways. After the Civil War started, Douglass fought for the right of African Americans to enlist and fight in the Union army. After the war he worked to get African Americans the right to vote.

spirits and black spirits engaged in battle, and the sun was darkened—the thunder rolled in the Heavens, and blood flowed in streams."

On the night of August 21, 1831, Turner and six of his followers walked to the Travis house, where Turner's master slept. They killed the entire family in their beds. Then they started going from house to house, killing all of the white people they found and encouraging their slaves to join them. Turner and about 40 other slaves then headed toward the town of Jerusalem, Virginia. By the time the Virginia state militia caught up with them, about 60 white men, women, and children had been clubbed, stabbed, and shot to death. The state of Virginia executed 55 men in connection with the revolt, including Nat Turner.

The violence didn't end with Turner, unfortunately. Mass hysteria followed the rebellion. As many as 200 slaves were massacred by mobs of panicked whites, who feared that all slaves would revolt. Southern states quickly passed new laws and tightened the restrictions used to control slaves. Turner's revolt made it more difficult for slaves to gather, travel, or be educated. Previously, slaves could carry weapons if their owners allowed it. New laws banned this. In addition, any slave accused of plotting rebellion was put to death.

A dozen years after Nat Turner's revolt, Henry Highland Garnet stood before the delegates of the 1843 National Negro Convention in Buffalo, New York. Garnet had escaped slavery as a young man and had become a respected abolitionist and Presbyterian minister. In his speech at the previous year's convention, he'd said that freedom for slaves should come through political change. He thought that whites needed to be convinced of the evils of slavery, then they'd change the laws and abolish slavery. But this year's convention audience heard a different message. Garnet had changed his mind. He now believed that slaves should be encouraged to turn on their masters and revolt. He said so in his "Call to Rebellion" speech.

✦✦ *Brethren, arise, arise! Strike for your lives and liberties. Now is the day and the hour. Let every slave throughout the land do this, and the days of slavery are numbered. You cannot be more oppressed than you have been—you cannot suffer greater cruelties than you have already. Rather die freemen than live to be slaves. Remember that you are FOUR MILLIONS! . . . Let your motto be resistance! resistance! RESISTANCE! No oppressed people have ever secured their liberty without resistance . . . Trust in the living God. Labor for the peace of the human race, and remember that you are FOUR MILLIONS.*

▨ HENRY HIGHLAND GARNET, an abolitionist and former slave, in his 1843 "Call to Rebellion" speech

FREDERICK DOUGLASS AND WILLIAM LLOYD GARRISON WERE AMONG THE "RADICAL" ABOLITIONISTS THROWN OUT OF THIS MEETING IN BOSTON (ABOVE). ▨ *UNCLE TOM'S CABIN* BECAME A BESTSELLER IN THE NORTH, BUT IT WAS BANNED AS ILLEGAL ANTISLAVERY PROPAGANDA IN THE SOUTH. SAMUEL GREEN (RIGHT) WAS A FREE BLACK WHO LIVED IN MARYLAND. HE WAS SENTENCED TO 10 YEARS IN JAIL AFTER A COPY OF THE BOOK WAS FOUND IN HIS HOME.

DAVID WALKER

(1785–1830)

DAVID WALKER was born in North Carolina to a free mother and a slave father. By law this made Walker a free black, but he had a deep sympathy for those unfortunate enough to not be born of free mothers. Walker's travels in the South as a young man and the books he read made him a fierce abolitionist.

Walker moved to Boston, where he could better express his abolitionist views. He opened a secondhand clothes store and began writing his famous pamphlet. "Walker's Appeal," published in 1829, argued that slavery needed to end immediately because it went against the laws of both God and civilized society. "Walker's Appeal" called upon black people to rise up against their oppressors, doing whatever was necessary to end slavery and racism. The violent "kill or be killed" message in Walker's pamphlet upset many abolitionists and terrified slave owners. Being caught with the pamphlet was a serious crime in much of the South. Walker distributed his controversial pamphlet by sewing it into the clothes of African American sailors who came into his store. Walker himself had a price on his head, and he died under mysterious circumstances three months after publishing a third edition of the pamphlet. Many believed he was poisoned.

were tired of waiting for the government to abolish slavery. Lectures, pamphlets, meetings, conventions, and talking didn't seem to be getting the job done. They desperately wanted to *do* something to help slaves be free—now.

Neither Underground nor Railroad

The goal of abolitionism was to make slavery illegal. It wasn't to help individual slaves escape. But as George Washington's letter of complaint (page 39) shows, there'd always been some people willing to put their beliefs into action. In fact, the year after Washington wrote that letter, a teenager in Pennsylvania began hiding and helping runaway slaves. Isaac T. Hopper was a young Quaker who had moved to Philadelphia in 1787 to apprentice as a tailor. He soon learned not only to sew suits, but to help slaves escape.

Hopper wasn't alone in his efforts. By 1800 many people were helping slaves reach freedom. Who those helpers were and the kind of help they gave differed from place to place. In the Southern slave states, it was mostly slaves who helped runaways passing through. They gave them food, and perhaps hid them in a cabin or barn. Once runaways crossed into free states, free blacks and other abolitionists aided

Frederick Douglass and other abolitionists at the convention spoke out against the violence in Garnet's "Call to Rebellion." Then it came time to vote on whether or not to officially agree with Garnet's speech. The delegates voted against it by only one vote. The close vote revealed how frustrated the black abolitionists were. Many abolitionists—black and white—

fugitive slaves and protected them from being recaptured. But by the early 1800s, secret societies were coming into shape. Networks of people, pathways, and places were developing. Fugitive slaves were being directed on to specific routes that led to safe houses, where they could find food, shelter, and safety. Slaves were escaping along the Underground Railroad.

◈◈◈ *I was born in Western Virginia, in the year 1835, and lived there as the slave of Benjamin Cooper until I was twenty-four years of age. When I was quite a lad my brothers were sold from me, and when I grieved for them, Cooper told me that when I grew to manhood I would forget that I ever had any brother. But then and there I resolved that, should I live to become a man, I would take my mother and sisters and find a home where we would be free . . . I resolved to find us a home in Canada, and, with the assistance of Almighty God, I started on the fourth Saturday night in October, 1859, at one o'clock. With my mother and two sisters I crossed the Ohio River, and took what is called the "Underground Railroad."*

▨ HENRY PARKER, a former slave who escaped

Life as a slave on a Virginia plantation was brutal in 1820. But a slave named Howard (whose last name is unknown) thought he'd found a way to be free. Belpre, Ohio, is just across the Ohio River from what was then Virginia, and is today West Virginia. A man from Belpre named Frank Curtis made a deal with Howard. Curtis bought Howard's freedom, and in return Howard agreed to work off his price on Curtis's farm. As a free black, Howard could now live in Ohio legally. But Howard had left a wife on the plantation. She soon ran away to join her husband. Now Howard's wife was a fugitive slave. Howard hid her as best he could

HERO OF FREEDOM

HENRY HIGHLAND GARNET

(1815–1882)

WHEN HENRY HIGHLAND GARNET was nine, his family escaped slavery in Maryland. Garnet's father wanted his family to be free. His own father had been a prince in West Africa before he was captured, sold into slavery, and shipped to America. Garnet's father took his family and escaped to Pennsylvania. From there, the Underground Railroad guided them to New York City.

Henry Garnet went to a school for free blacks in New York. He was an outstanding student, and he went on to become a Presbyterian minister and an abolitionist speaker. David Walker's (page 50) writings convinced Garnet to change his mind about how best to end slavery in America. He began to call on slaves to rise up and rebel.

After the Civil War, Garnet became the pastor of a church in Washington, D.C., that helped many poor African American soldiers. Later, he helped the U.S. government develop programs to aid former slaves. Garnet favored African American emigration to Africa. In 1881 the American Colonization Society appointed him U.S. minister to Liberia. He died there of fever.

ISAAC T. HOPPER.

near the farm. But soon her owner came over to Ohio to capture her. He'd figured she'd run away to be with her husband.

The owner captured Howard's wife near Curtis's farm. Howard was working in the field, and he saw her being taken back toward the Ohio River. He wasn't going to let his wife go back to the plantation and be punished for running away. Howard hid along the path to the river and waited. When the men passed by with his wife, Howard ambushed them with a club. The slave owner left Ohio without his runaway. But Howard and his wife knew that her owner would be back soon with a search party. The couple quickly left the farm and headed north. Frank Curtis wrote in a letter, "Howard ran with his wife on the Underground to Canada." It's one of the earliest recorded uses of "underground" to describe the secret network that helped escaping slaves.

Another early story tells of a slave named Tice Davids, who ran away from his Kentucky master in 1831. Davids made it across the Ohio River to Ripley, Ohio. Chasing him in a boat, his owner made it across the river to Ohio minutes later. But after searching the abolitionist town, Davids's master came up empty-handed. He gave up his search and is said to have declared that Davids "must have gone off on an underground road." In later years, as fast steam-engine railroads became more common, the story changed to Davids escaping on the "underground railroad." The name stuck because it fit. The networks of people, pathways, and safe houses had to be secret, or "underground," because it was a crime to give food, shelter, or assistance to a fugitive slave. And fugitives were moved northward along these networks quickly, like a fast train on a railroad track. The speedy and secret routes of the "underground railroad" protected fugitives from capture and their helpers from arrest.

I arrived at last at a large station of the "underground railway," about one hundred and sixty miles from the banks of the Ohio river. But my mind was not yet at rest. Two or three nights in succession I dreamed that I was recaptured by my master, all the details of the capture were so vividly depicted in my dreams, that I could scarcely believe when awake, that they were merely visions of the night.

Rev. Francis Frederick, a former slave who escaped from Virginia to Canada

Conductors, Agents, and Stationmasters

To help keep the people and places of the Underground Railroad secret, people often spoke or wrote using code words, which were copied from real train travel. Fugitive slaves were called "passengers," "travelers," "baggage," or "cargo." Sometimes, male fugitives were called "packages of hardware" and women were called "dry goods." "Conductors" were those who guided runaways to freedom. People who mapped out "routes," "arranged passage," and made sure the way was safe were called "agents." Cities or towns where fugitive slaves could get help along the way were called "terminals." Many well-traveled terminals had their own code names. Sandusky, Ohio, on the shore of Lake Erie, was called "Hope," for example. Safe houses, where runaways were sheltered, were called "stations." A person who owned or operated a safe house was called a "stationmaster." "Brakemen" helped fugitives start new lives in Northern states and in Canada.

◆◆ *Sir, I have just received a letter from my friend . . . in which he says, that by writing to you, I may get some information about the transportation of some property from this neighborhood to your city or vicinity . . . It is for the conveyance of only one small package; but it has been discovered since, that the removal cannot be so safely effected without taking two larger packages with it. I understand that the three are to be brought to this city and stored in safety, as soon*

as the forwarding merchant in Philadelphia shall say he is ready to send on.

▨ J. Bigelow, lawyer and Underground Railroad agent, writing in code to another agent about some fugitives

Underground Railroad conductors, agents, and stationmasters risked arrest, fines, and being jailed for the illegal activities they engaged in to help criminal fugitives. Most Americans—Northern and Southern—disapproved of the Underground Railroad. Underground Railroad workers were seen as lawbreaking troublemakers. Many Americans thought slavery was wrong. But few were going to break the law to help enslaved strangers escape.

So who were these agents, conductors, stationmasters, and brakemen that were willing to help? Many of their names are lost to history. They were, after all, breaking the law. Writing down who they helped and how might get them caught—so few kept records. Most slaves that rode the Underground Railroad kept their secrets to themselves, too. Telling where one stayed, or who assisted in one's journey, might help a slave catcher snag a future fugitive en route. But not all the names, places, and histories have been lost. Many Underground Railroad agents, conductors, stationmasters, and brakemen were

THIS PAGE FROM THE DIARY OF QUAKER STATIONMASTER DANIEL OSBORN IS A RARE RECORD OF SOME OF THE INDIVIDUALS WHO WERE SENT ALONG THE UNDERGROUND RAILROAD.

WRITE AND DECODE UNDERGROUND RAILROAD MESSAGES

WORKING IN OR TRAVELING the Underground Railroad was illegal. Escaping slaves and those who helped them were at constant risk of being caught. One way to hide what they were doing was to use code words and phrases when talking or sending messages. Use this Underground Railroad code dictionary to decode the letter written by J. Bigelow (see page 53). Then write your own letter in Underground Railroad code and ask a friend or family member to decode it.

UNDERGROUND RAILROAD CODE PHRASES

The Wind Blows from the South Today: An alert to Underground Railroad workers that runaway slaves are in the local area

When the Sun Comes Back and the First Quail Calls: A reminder that early spring is a good time of year to escape, because fugitives could travel north before it became cold in winter

The Riverbank Makes a Mighty Good Road: A reminder that bloodhounds can't follow scent through the water

The Dead Trees Will Show You the Way: A reminder that moss grows on the cooler north side of dead trees and can point the way northward

It's a Friend with Friends: A password used by an Underground Railroad conductor arriving at an Underground Railroad safe house with a group of fugitives

The Friend of a Friend Sent Me: A password used by a fugitive traveling without a conductor to signal an Underground Railroad stationmaster that he

or she was sent by the Underground Railroad.

Steal Away, Steal Away, Steal Away to Jesus: A way to let other slaves know that an escape attempt is coming up

The Train Is Off the Track: An alert that trouble has been encountered while transporting a runaway

Lost a Passenger: A term used to signal that a runaway slave has been recaptured

UNDERGROUND RAILROAD CODE DICTIONARY

Agent: A person who plots the course and makes arrangements for escaping fugitive slaves

Baggage: Escaping fugitive or runaway slaves

Brakeman: A person who helps fugitive slaves find work and homes once they are in free states or in Canada

Cargo: One or more fugitive or runaway slaves

Conductor: A person who guides slaves along their journey to freedom or who gives slaves directions on how to escape

Drinking Gourd: The Big Dipper star grouping, which points to the North Star

Forwarding: Transporting fugitive slaves from station to station

Freedom Line: An escaped slave's route of travel

Freedom Train: The Underground Railroad

Heaven: Canada

Hope: Sandusky, Ohio

Judgment Day: The day or time of escape

Load of Potatoes: A wagon full of fugitive slaves who are hidden under farm produce such as hay or potatoes

Moses: Harriet Tubman

Operator: An Underground Railroad worker

Parcel or Package: A fugitive or runaway slave who is traveling along the Underground Railroad

Passenger: A fugitive or runaway slave who is traveling along the Underground Railroad

Promised Land: Canada, or sometimes the North

Route: The escape route used by one or more runaways or fugitives

Shepherd: A person who escorts escaping slaves

Shipment: Arriving fugitive slaves

Station: A safe place where fugitives are sheltered

Stationmaster: A person who runs a safe house

Stockholder: A person who donates money, clothing, or food to the Underground Railroad

Terminal: A stop such as a town or a city on the Underground Railroad

Traveler: An escaping fugitive or runaway slave

abolitionists whose belief in their cause outweighed their fear of punishment. Most of the abolitionists mentioned in this book worked in the Underground Railroad—many as stationmasters—and their stories and experiences have survived.

The majority of Underground Railroad workers were African Americans, although white Americans also helped transport slaves to freedom. If escaping runaways received any help in the South at all—most reached the North on their own—it was usually from slaves they encountered on their way northward. Once they crossed into free states, free blacks provided much of the food, clothing, shelter, and support for escaping slaves. Free blacks working in hotels, train stations, and ports kept their eyes and ears open. When slave catchers and bounty hunters came into town, they quickly passed a warning along the Underground Railroad. Abolitionists of all races and well-to-do free blacks raised money to help fugitive slaves make it to freedom.

Most free blacks had very personal reasons for aiding fugitive slaves. Many had once been slaves themselves, or had relatives that had been or were currently enslaved. Even free blacks had to be wary of slave catchers and bounty hunters. The rising price for slaves made kidnapping free blacks to sell into slavery a profitable business. After 1850, the word of any white person claiming that an African American was a fugitive slave was accepted as true—unless another white person disagreed. Neither free nor enslaved blacks were allowed to speak in court against whites in many states. Free black children were especially vulnerable to kidnapping. Slave catchers quickly sold them to plantation owners in the Deep South, and they were never heard from again.

I was taken from [my employer] Joseph C. Miller's . . . by two men . . . One came in and . . . seized me by the arm, and pulled me out of the house. Mrs. Miller called to her husband, who was in the front porch, and he ran out and seized the man by the collar, and tried to stop him. The other, with an oath told him to take his hands off, and if he touched me he would kill him. He then told Miller that I belonged to Mr. Schoolfield, in Baltimore. They then hurried me to a wagon . . . I was taken to Baltimore . . . to jail. The next morning, a man with large light-colored whiskers took me by myself, and asked me if I was not Mr. Schoolfield's slave. I told him I was not; he said that I was, and that if I did not say I was he would "cowhide me and salt me, and put me in a dungeon." I told him I was free, and that I would say nothing but the truth.

▨ RACHEL PARKER, a free black recounting her 1851 kidnapping in Pennsylvania

JACOB C. WHITE (TOP) AND N. W. DEPEE (BOTTOM) WERE MEMBERS OF PHILADELPHIA'S BUSY GENERAL VIGILANCE COMMITTEE.

SINGING TO FREEDOM

RUNAWAY SLAVES heading toward freedom in Canada sometimes sang songs that contained coded messages, like the song that Harriet Tubman sang to her master's house slaves to let them know that she was fleeing slavery. Exhausted fugitives also sang songs to lift their spirits and remind them of why they were struggling to be free. The song "I'm on My Way to Canada" was sung to the tune of "Oh Susannah," a popular Southern song that includes the lyrics "Oh, Susannah, now don't you cry for me. For I've come from Alabama with a banjo on my knee." Gather up some friends or family and sing along.

"I'm on My Way to Canada"

I'm on my way to Canada,
That cold and dreary land;
The sad effects of slavery,
I can no longer stand.
I've served my master all my days,
Without a dime's reward;
And now I'm forced to run away,
To flee the lash abroad.

Farewell, old master, don't think hard of me,
I'm on my way to Canada, where all the slaves
are free.

The hounds are baying on my track,
Old master comes behind,
Resolved that he will bring me back,
Before I cross the line;
I'm now embarked for yonder shore,
There a man's a man by law;
The iron horse will bear me o'er,
To shake the lion's paw.

Oh, righteous Father, will thou not pity me,
And aid me on to Canada, where all the slaves
are free.

Oh, I heard Queen Victoria say,
That if we would forsake
Our native land of slavery,
And come across the lake;
That she was standing on the shore,
With arms extended wide,
To give us all a peaceful home
Beyond the rolling tide.

Farewell, old master, don't think hard of me,
I'm on my way to Canada, where all the slaves
are free.

To protect themselves from kidnapping and an unfair justice system, free blacks in Northern cities formed groups, which were often called vigilance committees. Vigilance committee members watched out for kidnappers and kept the free black community alert. But in many cities, including New York, Philadelphia, Boston, and Detroit, vigilance committees also sheltered and transported runaway slaves. While abolitionist societies were encouraging the public to turn against slavery, African American vigilance committees were getting slaves to freedom. Free black communities also provided many runaways with new homes. While some fugitives escaped to Canada, others changed their names and settled in free black communities in the North. Many of these former slaves, in turn, became workers on the Underground Railroad. Even free blacks in slave states helped, if they could. Jacob R. Gibbs was a free black who lived in Baltimore, Maryland—a slave state. He kept a file with the "free papers" of local free blacks who'd died. He handed out the papers to runaways, who used them to pass as free blacks as they traveled northward.

Tougher Laws

The Underground Railroad was secretive. But slave owners knew their runaways were getting help—and they didn't like it. They wanted laws that made it easier to recapture their runaways, and stiffer punishments for those helping fugitive slaves. The Fugitive Slave Law of 1850 delivered both. Under this law, no one who was accused of being a runaway slave was allowed a trial. Instead, suspected runaways were taken in front of a commissioner, who heard only the testimony of the owner before sending the fugitive back to slavery. Thousands of free blacks fled the North for Canada after the law was passed. Many were former slaves who'd escaped years ago. But they were less safe under the new law. Other free blacks fled to escape kidnapping, which the new law made even easier to get away with.

Many white Northerners also hated the Fugitive Slave Law of 1850, even though some of them were not necessarily against slavery. They believed that the new law abused their rights. The law made the federal government responsible for returning runaways. U.S. marshals could now legally burst into anyone's home without permission to look for fugitives. Federal marshals could also legally force citizens to help them capture fugitive slaves.

Supporters of the new Fugitive Slave Law wanted it to stop the Underground Railroad.

But just the opposite happened. It made the Underground Railroad stronger. Many Northern whites who had disapproved of the illegal activities of conductors and stationmasters now changed their minds. More people gave money to help fugitives. Lawyers offered to defend fugitives and those arrested for helping them. The number of "passengers" riding the Underground Railroad increased greatly after 1850, and so did the number of Underground Railroad workers. Many more runaways wanted to flee all the way to Canada now, where they could truly be free.

◈◈ *I determined to make my escape to Canada, about which I had heard something, as beyond the limits of the United States; for, notwithstanding there were free States in the Union, I felt that I should be safer under an entirely foreign jurisdiction. The slave States had their emissaries in the others, and I feared that I might fall into their hands, and need a stronger protection than might be afforded me by public opinion in the northern States at that-time.*

▨ REV. JOSIAH HENSON, a former slave and an Underground Railroad conductor

THE FUGITIVE SLAVE LAW OF 1850 INCREASED VIOLENT ENCOUNTERS BETWEEN ARMED SLAVE CATCHERS AND RUNAWAYS OR KIDNAPPED FREE BLACKS.

CHAPTER 3

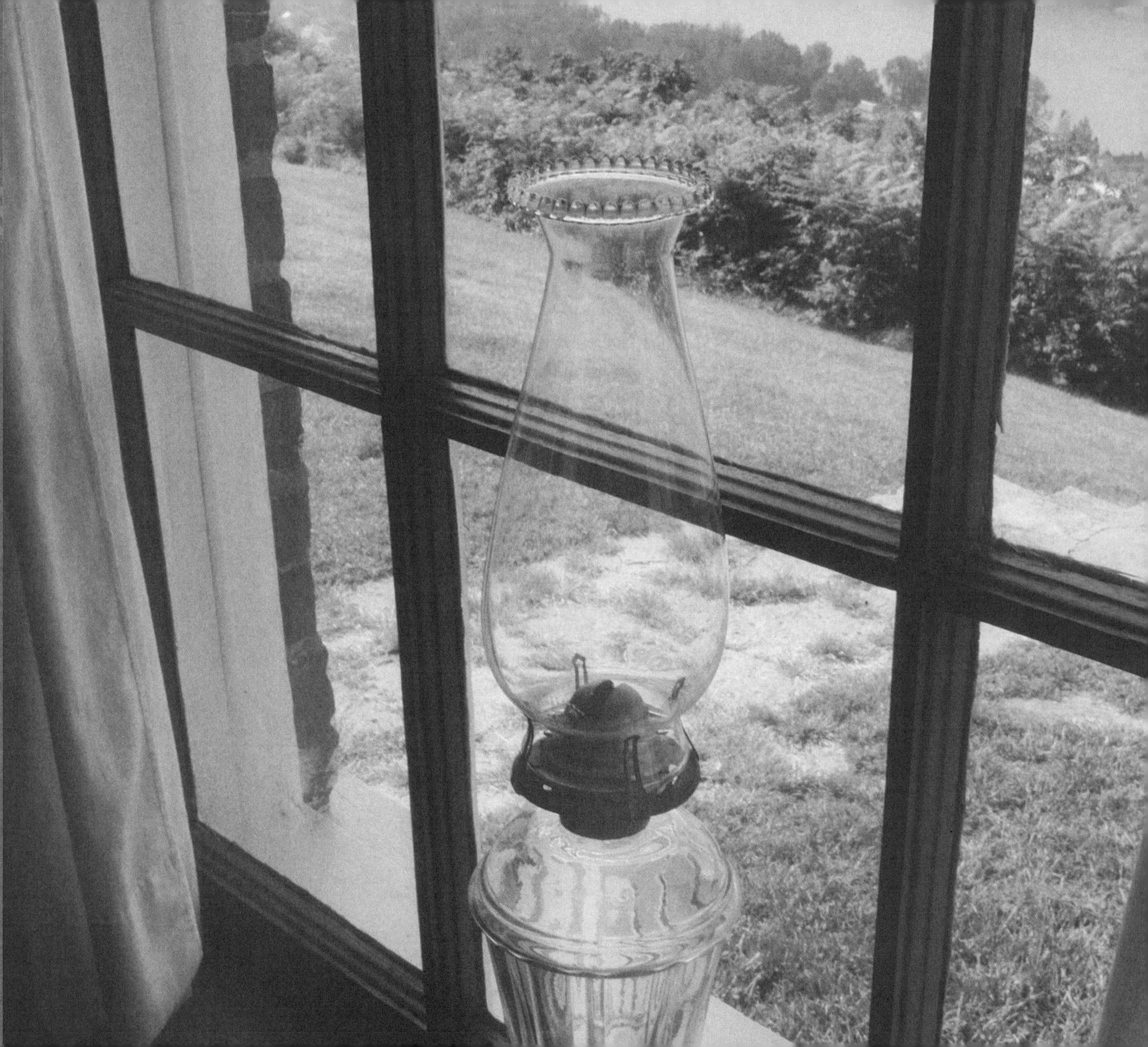

Conductors

Transporting Illegal Cargo

IN 1850, after living in the North for only a year, Harriet Tubman began putting her own freedom at risk to help other slaves escape. She'd saved up some travel money. Now it was time to start rescuing her family from slavery. They deserved to be free, too. Harriet decided to start with her sister Mary Ann and her two young children. Mary Ann was a house slave who was married to a free black man named John Bowley. Harriet couldn't read or write herself, so she had someone else write a letter to Bowley. The letter from Harriet suggested a way for his wife and children to escape.

The plan was for Bowley to hire a boat in nearby Cambridge, Maryland, that would take his family up the Chesapeake Bay to Baltimore, Maryland. Harriet would cross back over into the slave state and meet them there on a set date. Their plans nearly fell through, however, when Mary Ann's master suddenly decided to sell her—on the very day of her planned escape! Mary Ann was taken to Cambridge and auctioned off to a new owner. But she managed to escape while the auctioneer was at lunch. John Bowley rushed Mary Ann and their children to the boat and headed toward Baltimore. Harriet met them there and successfully "conducted" them on to Philadelphia.

HARRIET TUBMAN.

Harriet snuck back into Maryland again the following year. This time she rescued her brother, John Ross, and two other slaves who wanted to escape. Harriet's third trip into Maryland was especially risky. She traveled back to her old home to ask her husband to come live with her in Philadelphia. There was a good chance that someone would recognize her and turn her in as a fugitive. When Harriet arrived back at her old home, her heart was crushed. John Tubman had remarried. But Harriet wouldn't let her risky trip into Maryland be for nothing. She easily found 10 slaves who wanted to run away, and she conducted them to freedom.

Harriet learned new tricks of the Underground Railroad–conducting trade with each trip South. Her rescue missions soon took on a successful pattern that allowed her to make 19 trips into the South without ever being caught—or losing a "passenger." She usually worked until she'd saved up enough money to provide for her passengers en route. Then she traveled south. Once in the South, Harriet gathered up her group of runaways and started them on their journey, often on a Saturday night. She knew that, because shops were closed and no newspapers were published on Sundays, slave owners would be unable to print up or publish advertisements about the runaways until

Monday. By then, Harriet and her passengers would have traveled northward for two full nights. The fleeing group usually hid in the woods during the day, often while Harriet went to look for food. She signaled whether it was safe or not by singing. If the hiding runaway slaves heard Harriet singing a sad song in the distance, they knew to stay hid and quiet. If they heard a joyful song, they knew they were safe—and that Harriet was on her way back to them.

Guides and Protectors

Harriet Tubman guided her human cargo from slave states in the eastern Upper South, such as Delaware and Maryland, to Philadelphia, Pennsylvania. Once in the free state of Pennsylvania, she often led fugitives on the Underground Railroad through New York and into Canada. This was one of the major Underground Railroad routes east of the Appalachian Mountains (see the map on facing page). Sometimes Tubman delivered her "passengers" to "stationmasters" in free states, who helped them along to their final destinations from there. Other times she guided runaways on safe routes to Canada herself, stopping at Underground Railroad stations only to rest.

The job of the conductors was to deliver runaways to safe Underground Railroad stations. Some, like Tubman, went into the South and led slaves out. But most conductors simply shuttled slaves from one station or safe house to another. Sometimes that meant taking them by boat across rivers, or simply walking with them on the safest route. Many conductors also carried fugitives in their wagons. Often the runaways were hidden under straw or a false bottom. Fugitive slaves might meet a chain of "conductors" as they traveled northward—each one guiding them from one station to the next.

With my mother and two sisters I crossed the Ohio River, and took what is called the "Underground Railroad." . . . *The first friend I found was a man whose name was Komines. He conducted us to the house of a colored man, whose name was John Williams, where we rested during the day; for we were compelled to travel at night and rest during the day. That night many friends came to our relief, and guided us for about twelve miles, when we met a company of twenty men who were friends to the cause of freedom, and who met us with a warm reception . . . Our friends left us one by one, but we met with another friend, whose name was Jonathan Lee. . . . We then traveled on until we reached Mr. Moses Clendennan's,*

ROUTES TO CANADA

There were two major Underground Railroad routes east of the Appalachian Mountains. One ran from the eastern Upper South through Philadelphia and New York State into Canada. The other route often involved stowing away on ships that were leaving southern East Coast towns such as Charleston, South Carolina, and Portsmouth, Virginia, and heading north. Once the ships docked in a northern city, such as New York City or New Bedford, Massachusetts, the fugitives made their way through

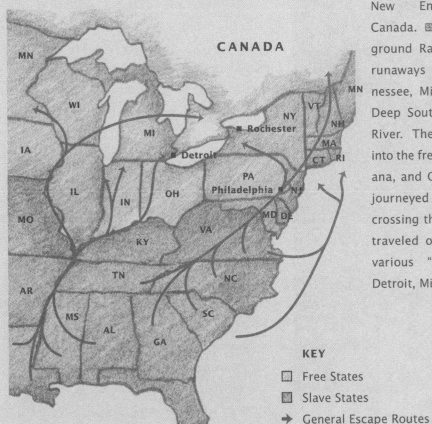

New England and into Canada. ⊞ The western Underground Railroad routes carried runaways out of Kentucky, Tennessee, Missouri, and even the Deep South via the Mississippi River. These fugitives crossed into the free states of Illinois, Indiana, and Ohio. From there they journeyed to Canada, often by crossing the Great Lakes. Others traveled over land, stopping in various "terminals," such as Detroit, Michigan, along the way.

KEY

▢ Free States

▨ Slave States

➔ General Escape Routes

MANY RUNAWAY SLAVES WALKED MOST OF THE WAY DURING THEIR JOURNEY TO FREEDOM. THEY FOLLOWED SECLUDED WOODED PATHS AT NIGHT.

another kind friend, and from thence to Mr. Dunlap's, where we were cordially received, and from there we were conveyed on from one kind friend to another until we reached Putnam, Ohio.

⊞ HENRY PARKER, a former slave who escaped from Virginia

✥ *At the age of sixteen I commenced my labors with the underground road. The way that we used to conduct the business was this: a white man would carry a certain number of slaves for a certain amount . . . We used to communicate with each other in this wise: one of us would go to the slaves and find out how many wanted to go, and then we would inform the party who was to take them, and some favorable night they would meet us out in the woods; we would then blow a whistle, and the man in waiting would answer "all right;" he would then take his load and travel by night, until he got into a free State. Then I have taken a covered wagon, with as many as fourteen in, and if I met any one that asked me where I was going, I told them that I was going to market. I became so daring, that I went within twenty miles of Elkton [Maryland]. At one time the kidnappers were within one mile of me; I turned the corner of a house, and went into some bushes, and that was the last they saw of me.*

⊞ JAMES WILLIAMS, an Underground Railroad conductor and former slave

Instructors in Escape

Not all Underground Railroad conductors were guides. Some simply passed on information to runaway slaves, instructing them where to go for help. A conductor in a slave state might tell slaves how to find a safe house just across the border, give advice on the safest route, or pass along the name of a nearby stationmaster. But it was up to the slaves themselves to take the first step.

Alexander Ross couldn't get the horrible slave auction out of his head. "The cries and heart-rending agonies of the poor creatures as they were sold and separated from parents, children, husbands, or wives, will never cease to ring in my ears," wrote Ross. "Babes were torn from the arms of their mothers and sold, while parents were separated and sent to distant parts of the country." Ross was a doctor from Belleville, Ontario, in Canada. He witnessed the slave auction while in New Orleans, Louisiana. Ross decided he wanted to help slaves escape, and he came up with a plan. Ross was an enthusiastic bird watcher, and he began traveling to plantations in the Deep South with the excuse of looking for birds. Most plantation owners were flattered that such an educated man wanted to visit their property. They eagerly allowed him onto their land and let him choose slaves as guides for his hikes.

CANDLE IN A CUP

THERE WERE NO flashlights during Underground Railroad times. But Harriet Tubman and other conductors sometimes carried the next-best thing—cups with candles inside them. Make your own to-go cup candle in this activity.

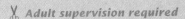 *Adult supervision required*

YOU'LL NEED

- ⊠ Empty aluminum soup can
- ⊠ Saucepan
- ⊠ Water
- ⊠ Knife
- ⊠ 3–5 ounces (85–140 gm) paraffin candle wax or old candles
- ⊠ 8 to 10 inches (21 to 26 cm) of candle wicking
- ⊠ Pencil or craft stick
- ⊠ Old teacup or coffee mug
- ⊠ Oven mitt
- ⊠ Scissors

1. Remove and discard the lid and label of the can. Clean it and let it air dry, being careful of its sharp edges.

2. Fill a saucepan with a few inches of water and bring to a simmer over medium heat.

3. While the water is heating, use the knife to cut up the paraffin or old candles into chunks. Fill the dry can with wax chunks.

4. Set the wax-filled can into the simmering pan of water. Let the wax melt. Add more water to the pan if needed.

5. While the wax is melting, tie one end of the candle wicking to the middle of the pencil or craft stick

6. Put the other end of the candle wicking into the teacup or mug, and set the pencil or craft stick across the cup's rim. Make sure the candle wicking hangs straight down into the center of the teacup or mug. You can trim off the end of the candle wicking if it's too long to hang straight.

7. Once the wax has completely melted, put on the oven mitt. Using the hand that's covered by the oven mitt, carefully pick up the can and slowly pour the wax into the cup. Don't worry if some wax gets on the pencil or wick. Check to make sure the candle wicking still hangs straight down into the center of the teacup or mug. Let the wax cool.

8. After your candle has cooled and become solid, use scissors to cut the candlewick away from the pencil. Trim the candlewick so it's about a half-inch (1 cm) long. Your candle is ready to use!

! BE SAFE: Never leave a lighted candle unattended.

Ross told those slaves about the freedom that awaited them in Canada. If they were interested in trying to escape, he gave them advice. One Mississippi slave named Joe (last name unknown) told Ross that he planned to escape very soon. "I gave him instructions for his guidance after he should cross the Ohio river; the names of friends at Evansville (Indiana), and Cleveland (Ohio), to whom he could apply for assistance," Ross wrote. "I also furnished him with a pistol, knife, and pocket compass, and directed him to travel by night until he reached friends north of the Ohio river." Joe soon ran away with his brother, who lived on a nearby plantation.

Joe's master discovered that Joe was missing and suspected that Ross had helped him. The Canadian doctor was charged with being an abolitionist who aided runaways. Ross was handcuffed and put in jail, where he awaited trial. He was sure he'd be convicted and sent to prison. On the day of the trial, Joe's owner made his case before the judge. The judge turned to ask Ross if he had anything to say in his defense. Suddenly a man burst into the courtroom. It was Joe himself! Joe explained to his owner that he hadn't really run away. He'd just gone to visit his brother and had fallen ill for a few days. The slave owner apologized to Ross, and in return Ross asked that Joe not be punished. Ross knew that Joe was lying to pro-

tect him. Joe had postponed his own freedom to save Ross from prison.

Two years later, Ross was eating in a Boston restaurant. A waiter came up to him and asked if he remembered him. Ross realized that it was Joe! Joe told Ross the story of his escape from Columbus, Mississippi, with his brother a few days after Ross's trial. This is how Ross recounted it: "At midnight they started together, moving as rapidly as they could through the fields and woods, keeping the north star in front of them. Whenever it was possible they walked in the creeks and marshy grounds, to throw the slave-hunters off their tracks. Thus, night after night, they kept on their weary way, hungry and sorefooted. On the morning of the seventeenth day of their freedom, they reached the Ohio river . . . All day they lay secreted in the bushes, at night they crossed the river in a small boat, and traveled rapidly, taking a north-easterly course. After enduring many hardships, they reached Cleveland, Ohio, and went to the house of a friend whose name I had given Joe. They were there kindly received, and supplied with clothing and other comforts. Resting a week, they were sent on to Canada, where Joe's brother still lives."

Other conductors traveled to the South to instruct slaves on escaping to Canada. Some posed as traveling salesmen. The famous abolitionist and conductor Laura Smith Haviland

THE IMAGE OF A YOUNG MALE RUNAWAY SLAVE HURRYING NORTHWARD, HIS FEW BELONGINGS TIED TO A STICK AND CARRIED OVER HIS SHOULDER, BECAME A SYMBOL OF THE ANTISLAVERY MOVEMENT IN AMERICA.

(see page 66) even pretended to be a berry picker. This got her into plantation kitchens, where house slaves worked. From there she was able to pass on information to slaves about where they could find help escaping. Like Tubman, Haviland also personally led escaping slaves out of the South, and she worked closely with stationmasters.

✦ *About three o'clock in the morning my mother and sisters' physical powers failed them, and we were compelled to rest at a colored man's house, whose name was William Mailes. Mother and sisters rested there the remainder of the night, but Mr. Mailes conducted me to the house of a friend, two miles distant, whose name was Brown. We all remained in this condition until the next night, when my mother and sisters joined me about nine o'clock. They were brought in a two-horse vehicle. We traveled on until about twelve o'clock of the same night, when we reached the house of a Quaker, where we had what was called "a midnight supper;" and when he sat down to the table, with a smile on his pleasant face, he said: "I'll take thee in, I'll feed thee, and I'll travel with thee, but thee must do thy own fighting, as we Quakers never fight." I replied that I trusted in God, and that he had promised to fight all our battles for us.*

▨ HENRY PARKER, a former slave who escaped from Virginia along the Underground Railroad

PACK UP AND GO

RUNAWAY SLAVES had few possessions, including suitcases. But a long, straight pole of wood made both a good walking stick and a weapon that could be used in case of attack by bloodhounds. If runaways did have some extra food or clothing to carry, they could tie it up in a cloth or shirt and use the stick to carry their bundle. See for yourself if carrying a load is easier when it's hung on a stick.

YOU'LL NEED
⊠ Large bandana or other 2-foot-by-2-foot (60-cm-by-60-cm) square piece of fabric
⊠ Broomstick, yardstick, or other thick, long stick
⊠ Portable snacks
⊠ Old shirt of any kind

1. Lay the bandana or fabric out flat on the floor.
2. Place your snacks and shirt in the middle of the bandana.
3. Take two opposite corners of the bandana and tie them once. Repeat with the remaining two corners, so that all of the tied corners meet in the middle of the bandana or fabric.
4. Set one end of the stick on top of the tied corners. Wrap the tied corners over the stick and tie them in a knot.

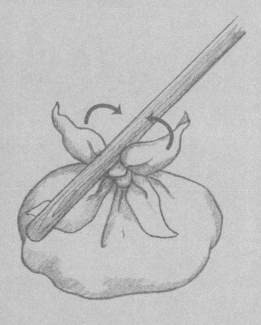

5. Place the stick and its baggage over your shoulder and go for a walk. How easy is it to transport your possessions this way?

Safe Havens and Safe Houses

Conductors and stationmasters on the Underground Railroad had the same goal. They wanted to help slaves be free from slavery. The job of the stationmasters was to provide a safe haven for runaways as they traveled north. Fugitive slaves were pursued by their owners, slave patrols, local lawmen, and professional slave catchers. Underground Railroad stations gave slaves on the run a place to rest and hide during the day. On well-traveled routes there was often an Underground Railroad station about every 10 to 12 miles (16 to 19 kilometers). That is the distance most runaways could cover in a night of walking. But passengers on the Underground Railroad also traveled by wagon, boat, horseback, or even train to the next station. Quite a few stationmasters also worked as conductors, personally transporting the runaways as they traveled, and aiding in daring rescues.

Stationmasters and conductors helped smuggle their "cargo" northward as well. Fugitive slaves were hidden among actual cargo or livestock on trains, often with the help of sympathetic railway workers. A few slaves were even smuggled out of the South by being shipped in boxes! A great many runaways stowed away on riverboats and steamships. Captain Fountain was a sea captain who hid fugitive slaves below deck in a secret compartment. He transported at least 50 runaways from Virginia to Philadelphia, Pennsylvania. One time, the police boarded his ship to look for fugitives. They chopped at the deck with axes, but they didn't discover the secret hold full of human cargo.

HERO OF FREEDOM
LAURA SMITH HAVILAND
(1808–1898)

LAURA SMITH HAVILAND was born into a New England Quaker family. She married and moved with her husband to a farm in Michigan. Haviland helped organize the first antislavery society in Michigan, and she became a minister in the Wesleyan Methodist Church. Haviland and her husband soon opened the River Raisin Institute on their farm. It was a school that was open to all children—boys and girls, black and white. The Havilands were also Underground Railroad stationmasters, and they hid fleeing fugitives on their farm.

After the tragic deaths of Haviland's husband, her parents, a sister, and her youngest child during an epidemic, Laura Smith Haviland left the work of the River Raisin Institute to others and became a full-time Underground Railroad conductor. She worked with the Coffins (see page 102) in Indiana and Ohio, and she traveled into the South to help slaves escape to freedom. Haviland's success as a conductor earned her a $3,000 bounty for her capture. Haviland also spoke at antislavery meetings and taught at schools for free black children in Ohio and Canada. After the Civil War, Haviland worked to help freed slaves and orphaned children.

FIFTEEN FUGITIVE SLAVES ESCAPED ON THIS SCHOONER FROM NORFOLK, VIRGINIA, TO LEAGUE ISLAND, NEAR PHILADELPHIA, PENNSYLVANIA.

$40 REWARD—Ran away from my residence, near Mobile, two negro men, Isaac and Tim. Isaac is from 25 to 30 years old, dark complexion, scar on the right side of the head, and also one on the right side of the body, occasioned by buck shot. Tim is 22 years old, dark complexion, scar on the right cheek, as also another on the back of the neck. Captains and owners of steamboats, vessels, and water crafts of every description, are cautioned against taking them on board, under the penalty of the law, and all other persons against harboring or in any manner favoring the escape of said negroes, under like penalty.

—SARAH WALSH

FROM THE MONTGOMERY, ALABAMA, *MONTGOMERY ADVERTISER*, SEPTEMBER 29, 1837

[M]y thoughts were eagerly feasting upon the idea of freedom, when the idea suddenly flashed across my mind of shutting myself up in a box, and getting myself conveyed as dry goods to a free state. . . . The box which I had procured was three feet one inch wide, two feet six inches high, and two feet wide: and on the morning of the 29th day of March, 1849, I went into the box—having previously bored three gimlet holes opposite my face, for air, and provided myself with a bladder of water . . . [M]y friends nailed down the lid and had me conveyed to the Express Office . . . I had no sooner arrived at the office than I was turned heels up . . . I was then put upon a waggon and driven off to the depôt with my head down. . . . I was only twenty seven hours in the box, though travelling a distance of three hundred and fifty miles. I was then placed on a waggon and conveyed to the house where my friend in Richmond had arranged I should be received . . . The joy of

THE MAYOR AND POLICE OF NORFOLK, VIRGINIA, CHOPPED AT THE DECK OF CAPTAIN FOUNTAIN'S (FAR LEFT) SCHOONER, BUT THEY NEVER DISCOVERED THE 28 FUGITIVE SLAVES HIDDEN BELOW.

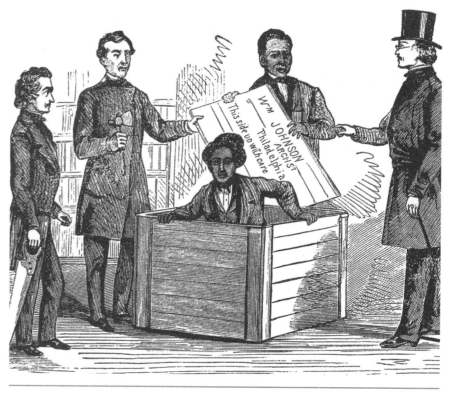

HENRY BROWN, A SLAVE, HAD HIMSELF SHIPPED IN A WOODEN CRATE TO AN ABOLITIONIST IN PHILADELPHIA.

the friends was very great; when they heard that I was alive they soon managed to break open the box, and then came my resurrection from the grave of slavery. I rose a freeman.

⊠ HENRY "BOX" BROWN, a former slave who escaped from Virginia and became a popular abolitionist speaker

Stationmasters also often fed and clothed fugitives and helped them on to their next route northward. Many stationmasters opened their own homes to runaways. Others allowed fugitive slaves to stay in their barns or cellars.

Eliza Harris was a runaway Kentucky slave who was desperately trying to reach the safety of an Underground Railroad station. She'd been told that a "good man" lived in the house on top of the cliff just across the Ohio River in Ripley, Ohio. But how could Harris get across the river? She'd fled her owner with her baby when she'd found out she was to be sold, thinking that she could walk across the Ohio River. It was wintertime, and ice often covered the water. But as she now stood by the river's edge, she was horrified. The ice had broken up, and huge chunks floated along in the water. Harris decided to wait until the ice became solid again. She left the riverbank to seek shelter for the night—then she saw the slave catchers heading her way.

Harris quickly ran back to the riverbank. She decided to try to cross the river. No matter how dangerous it was, it couldn't be worse than being caught. Wrapping her baby in a shawl and tying it around her neck, Harris stepped out onto the ice. She quickly jumped from one moving chunk of ice to another, sometimes slipping and falling into the frigid water. When a chunk of ice sank underneath her, Harris had to put her baby on the next block of ice and then pull herself up onto it. Harris and her baby, soaked to the skin and numb with cold, finally reached the Ohio shore. A man had seen her struggling across the ice. He helped her up the riverbank and pointed her toward Rev. John Rankin's house. She trudged up the long stairway that scaled the cliff to the Rankin home.

Harris found an unlocked door and was able to make a fire and warm herself and her baby.

HERO OF FREEDOM
REV. JOHN RANKIN
(1793–1886)

JOHN RANKIN was born in Tennessee, a slave state. His antislavery beliefs began early. Rankin founded an antislavery society in Kentucky while serving there as a young Presbyterian minister. His abolitionist views soon caused trouble for Rankin in the slave states, and in 1822 he moved his family across the Ohio River to the town of Ripley in the free state of Ohio. John Rankin was the minister of Ripley's Presbyterian Church for 44 years. During that time, the Rankin's house became an Underground Railroad station on one of the busiest routes out of the South.

The Rankins put a lit lamp in the upstairs window when it was safe for fugitive slaves to cross the Ohio River and come up the long stairway from the river to the house. The lit lamp in their house, which overlooks the Ohio River, could be seen from the Kentucky side at night. John Rankin, his wife, Jean, and their 13 children helped some 2,000 runaway slaves to freedom. "My house has been the door of freedom to many human beings, but while there was a hazard of life and property, there was much happiness in giving safety to the trembling fugitives," wrote Rankin.

THE HOME OF REV. RANKIN ATOP LIBERTY HILL (ABOVE) CAN STILL BE SEEN WHILE CROSSING THE OHIO RIVER TO RIPLEY, OHIO. A LONG FLIGHT OF STEPS LEADS FROM THE OHIO RIVER UP TO THE HOME OWNED BY THE STATION- MASTER REV. JOHN RANKIN (TOP RIGHT). A LAMP (RIGHT) LIKE THE ONE LIT BY THE RANKINS SITS IN A WINDOW WITH THE RIVER IN THE DISTANCE.

The Rankins were happy to help Eliza Harris. But they knew she wasn't safe there. Slave catchers had seen her cross the river, and they would soon be on their way to Ripley, Ohio, from Kentucky. Harris and her child were taken to a nearby Underground Railroad station before daylight. From there, they were passed on from one station to another. One of the Underground Railroad stations where Harris spent time was the home of Quakers Levi and Catherine Coffin in Newport, Indiana. These famous stationmasters helped Harris and her baby reach Canada, as they did hundreds of other runaways.

◈ *We knew not what night or what hour of the night we would be roused from slumber by a gentle rap at the door. That was the signal announcing the arrival of a train of the Underground Railroad . . . I have often been awakened by this signal, and sprang out of bed in the dark and opened the door. Outside in the cold or rain, there would be a two-horse wagon loaded with fugitives, perhaps the greater part of them women and children. I would invite them, in a low tone, to come in, and they would follow me into the darkened house without a word, for we knew not who might be watching and listening. When they were all safely inside and the door fastened, I would cover the windows, strike a light and build a good fire. By this time my wife would be up and preparing victuals for them, and in a short time the cold and hungry fugitives would be made comfortable.*

🔲 LEVI COFFIN, an Underground Railroad stationmaster

Willing Spirits and Good Souls

Eliza Harris was relieved to reach Canada, but she wasn't content there. She'd had to leave her other five children behind when she fled. They were still Kentucky slaves. Harris vowed to the Rankins that cold night she crossed the Ohio River that she'd be back. One day the following June, a "man" arrived at the Rankin's home. It was Harris in disguise! The Rankins helped Harris cross the river into Kentucky. She made her way back on her old plantation, where she hid in the bushes until she spotted her eldest daughter. Harris's daughter gathered up her brothers and sisters, and they and their mother headed out for the river at night. After an 11-mile (18-kilometer) walk, the family reached the Ohio River on a foggy morning. But the boat wasn't there!

"That morning," recounted Rev. Rankin, "when we expected to have Eliza and her children safe in Ohio, after the fog lifted, we saw 31 men on horseback with dogs and guns, across

the river hunting Eliza and her children, seeking the reward of $1,300." Harris and her children waded into the shallow water to try to throw the slave catchers' bloodhounds off their scent. Meanwhile, Reverend Rankin crossed the river into Kentucky a few miles upstream and put on a slave woman's clothes. Rankin tricked the slave hunters into following him instead of Harris and her children! A boatman was finally able to get to the family and ferry them across the river to Ohio. After hiding with the Rankins for a while, Harris and her five rescued children made it to Canada on the Underground Railroad.

Like Harriet Tubman, Eliza Harris had become an Underground Railroad conductor for very personal reasons. Both women were former slaves who desperately wanted to free their own families from slavery. Most Underground Railroad conductors and stationmasters were former slaves and free blacks who were determined to help free their people. But one often overlooked group who worked faithfully as Underground Railroad conductors and stationmasters were slaves themselves. In the South, there was little organized help for fleeing runaways. It was Southern slaves who hid runaways in their cabins and shared their scarce food with them.

Arnold Gragston was a Kentucky slave who rowed fugitives across the river for years.

VISIT AN UNDERGROUND RAILROAD STATION

AS YOU CAN SEE from the map on page 61, runaway slaves traveled through many parts of the United States and Canada. Find out if there's a house or other place near you that once sheltered escaping slaves.

If you have access to the Internet, start your search by checking out the Web sites listed on page 159. Many list Underground Railroad sites by state, with information on how to visit them. Another way to find out about Underground Railroad history in your area is to call or write to your town's, city's, or county's historical society or visitors bureau. Many public libraries also have this information. Happy hunting!

Gragston and his wife finally had to flee to the North when he was nearly caught helping fellow slaves. Richard Daly was another slave who conducted runaways across the river. When Daly's wife died, her master decided to sell the oldest of the Daly's four children. Daly quickly made his own decision. He took his children and fled to Canada on the Underground Railroad he'd helped run.

✥ *[As a slave] I had for years belonged to the underground railroad, and had helped about thirty slaves to escape. They would come from some of the counties in Kentucky back of the river, and send word to me beforehand. I would meet them about two miles above Milton, Ky., on the river bank at night, and row them over in a boat. I would fire my revolver when I was crossing the Ohio River, and my white friend, who was an agent of the underground railroad, would fire his revolver to say he was ready. Then I would land the fugitives, and he would take care of them and pass them along the road to Canada.*

▣ RICHARD DALY, a former slave and Underground Railroad conductor

Conductors and stationmasters—white and black—came from all walks of life. Some were wagon drivers who were willing to shuttle fugitives, or steamboat workers who were able to smuggle runaways aboard ship. Others were farmers whose rural homes lay along a northward Underground Railroad route. Many of the people who helped runaways were simply sympathetic strangers who were willing to give a runaway a meal, point out directions, or not alert the sheriff when they discovered a fleeing slave sleeping in a barn. A great number of Underground Railroad conductors and stationmasters were women. Most lawmen and slave catchers thought women weren't clever enough or bold enough to help fugitives. Their prejudice helped women such as Laura Haviland, Harriet Tubman, and Lucretia Mott avoid arrest. Henrietta Bowers Duterte was the first female African American undertaker in Philadelphia, Pennsylvania. She used her occupation to help fugitives, too. Duterte hid fugitives from slave hunters in caskets and among funeral processions.

Why were these "employees of the Underground Railroad" willing to risk fines and jail to help strangers? Many had once been slaves or had family that was still enslaved—what better reason was there? A great many were also abolitionists who were frustrated with trying to get the U.S. government to outlaw slavery. They wanted slaves to have immediate freedom. Many of the abolitionists mentioned in chapter 2, including William Wells Brown, Frederick Douglass, Harriet Beecher Stowe, Lucretia

Mott, and Jermain Wesley Loguen, were also Underground Railroad stationmasters, conductors, and agents. Certain religious groups, such as the Quakers and the Presbyterians, actively organized relief and safe houses for runaways. The Mount Zion United Methodist Church in Washington, D.C., ran an Underground Railroad station, hiding fugitive slaves in the burial vault of their African American cemetery. And Jewish members of the Touro Synagogue in Newport, Rhode Island, also sheltered fugitives.

After I had tasted the blessings of freedom, my mind reverted to those whom I knew were groaning in captivity, and I at once proceeded to take measures to free as many as I could. I thought that . . . numbers might make their escape as I did, if they had some practical advice how to proceed. I was once attending a very large meeting at Fort Erie [in Canada], at which a great many coloured people were present. In the course of my preaching, I tried to impress upon them the importance of the obligations they were under . . . to do all that was in their power to bring others out of bondage. In the congregation was a man named James Lightfoot . . . He then informed me where he came from, also to whom he belonged, and that he had left behind a dear father and mother, three sisters and four brothers; and that they lived on

LUCRETIA MOTT
(1793–1880)

LUCRETIA MOTT was born into a Quaker family in Massachusetts. She learned to speak out at Quaker meetings, and she became a minister at age 28. Like many Quakers, Mott believed that slavery was sinful and needed to be abolished. Mott was inspired to become active in the antislavery movement after meeting William Lloyd Garrison in 1830. In a time when women were often unwelcome at public meetings, Mott wanted to include women in abolitionism. In 1837 she helped found the Philadelphia Female Anti-Slavery Association. Lucretia Mott served as the organization's president for 40 years. The Philadelphia home of Mott and her husband, James, was also an Underground Railroad station. They sheltered and hid runaways in their home until the beginning of the Civil War. After the war, they worked to improve education for African Americans and for their right to vote.

Lucretia Mott was not only an outspoken abolitionist; she was also a leader for women's rights. Mott traveled to England for the World Anti-Slavery Convention in 1840. But the men who ran the convention wouldn't let any of the women delegates take part in the proceedings. The insult inspired Mott to work for women's rights, and she went on to help plan a women's rights convention in Seneca Falls, New York, in 1848. At this historic meeting, Mott, Elizabeth Cady Stanton, and other women's rights leaders wrote the Declaration of Sentiments. The document stated their goals for women's rights and laid the groundwork for women's suffrage, or right to vote.

the Ohio River, not far from the city of Maysville [Kentucky] . . . Seeing the agony of his heart in behalf of his kindred, I consented to commence the painful and dangerous task of endeavouring to free those whom he so much loved.

⊠ REV. JOSIAH HENSON, a former slave, recollecting his first mission as an Underground Railroad conductor

John Fairchild was an Underground Railroad conductor who started helping runaways for moral reasons. But he probably kept at it because he liked the excitement! Fairchild was born into a family of slaveholders in Virginia. Like many sons and daughters of slave owners, he played with slave children when he was young. Most of these white children grew up to find nothing wrong with the fact that their childhood friends were enslaved while they were not. But when Fairchild reached manhood, he believed that his slave friend Bill (last name unknown) should be free. Bill and Fairchild made a plan. They left their homes separately, but met up later. Then they traveled to Ohio pretending to be master and slave. From Ohio, Fairchild went with Bill to Canada, where the freed slave settled permanently.

Fairchild returned to Virginia to discover that his uncle suspected him of helping Bill run off. Fairchild decided to move to the North for good—and he took several more slaves with him! Fairchild was soon making regular trips into Southern states to conduct slaves out. He lived in Canada, and many fugitive slaves there hired him to go into the South to rescue their family members. Fairchild's southern accent helped him pose as a slave trader, slave owner, or salesman, and he usually moved throughout the South undetected. He was shot once and put in jail a number of times. But it's estimated that, over the course of 12 years, he delivered 1,500 runaways to Detroit, Michigan, on the Canadian border.

Partners in Crime

Another swashbuckling Underground Railroad conductor was John Parker. Parker was born a slave, but he had been able to buy his freedom (see facing page). As a free black, he'd moved to the river boomtown of Ripley, Ohio, to start a foundry—and to work on the Underground Railroad. Ripley was also the home of the Rankin family, who helped Eliza Harris. Parker and the Rankins worked together to get many hundreds of fugitive slaves across the Ohio River from Kentucky and on to Underground Railroad stations in Ohio. At that time, Ripley was a dangerous town filled with slave hunters, runaways, and Underground

Railroad workers. While Southerners called Ripley "an abolitionist hellhole," there were plenty of slavery supporters in town, too. Men on both sides of the slavery issue went around armed, and shots were often fired in the fight over fugitive slaves.

❧ *[F]ierce passions swept this little town, dividing its people into bitter factions. I never thought of going uptown without a pistol in my pocket, a knife in my belt, and a blackjack [club] handy. Day or night I dare not walk on the sidewalks for fear someone might leap out of a narrow alley at me . . . This was a period when men went armed with pistol and knife and used them on the least provocation. When under cover of night the uncertain steps of slaves were heard quietly seeking their friends. When the mornings brought strange rumors of secret encounters the night before, but daylight showed no evidence of the fray; when pursuers and pursued stood at bay in a narrow alley with pistols drawn ready for the assault; when angry men surrounded one of the houses . . .[and] kept up gunfire until late in the afternoon, endeavoring to break into it by force, in search of runaways. These were the days of passion and battle which turned father against son, and neighbor against neighbor.*

▣ JOHN PARKER, an inventor, Underground Railroad conductor, and former slave

JOHN P. PARKER

(1827–1900)

JOHN P. PARKER was born a slave in Virginia. When he was eight years old, Parker was sold away from his mother to a slave trader. Young Parker was chained to other slaves in a horrific coffle and marched from Virginia to Alabama. A doctor bought Parker, who learned to read and write from the physician's sons. Parker tried to escape a number of times as a teenager. But he was found and returned to his owner each time. Parker's master hired him out to work as a plasterer and an ironworker, and Parker soon became a skilled tradesman. He was eventually able to earn enough to buy his freedom at age 18.

Once a free man, Parker found work in iron foundries in Indiana and Ohio. He eventually married and settled in Ripley, Ohio, where he started his own foundry. Parker grew into a well-to-do businessman and inventor. John P. Parker invented several pieces of farm equipment, including a tobacco press and a soil pulverizer (see page 76). He was one of only a few African Americans who were granted U.S. patents in the 1800s.

Parker led something of a double life. He ran a successful business by day, but on many nights he armed himself with pistols and a knife and took his boat across the Ohio River to conduct runaways out of Kentucky. Parker was a daring Underground Railroad conductor who helped many hundreds of runaways to freedom. During the Civil War, Parker helped recruit black soldiers for the Union army, and his foundry made castings for the war effort.

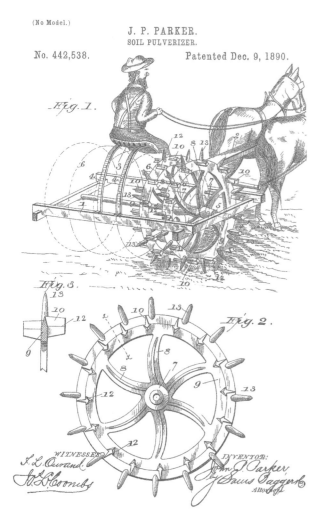

(No Model.)

J. P. PARKER.
SOIL PULVERIZER.

No. 442,538.   Patented Dec. 9, 1890.

JOHN PARKER INVENTED A NUMBER OF FARM TOOLS, INCLUDING THIS SOIL PULVERIZER (LEFT). AN IRON WHEEL (ABOVE) FROM THAT INVENTION SITS IN FRONT OF THE PARKER HOUSE IN RIPLEY, OHIO, TODAY.

The Reverend Rankin's sons woke John Parker from his Sunday sleep early one summer morning. There was urgent trouble: five runaways were gathered on the Kentucky side of the Ohio River, waiting to be taken across the river to freedom. But it was now broad daylight, and the fugitives could be clearly seen from the Ohio riverbank. "Seeing the fugitives aroused Rev. Rankin to fever pitch of doing something to rescue the runaways," recounted Parker. The Rankin boys asked Parker to come help—and to bring all of his firearms. "I can still see the pale face of Rev. Rankin as he sat in the center of this council of war, arguing for his plan of rescue," remembered Parker. "I soon learned his plan was [to] take his six sons, myself, and any others who would join the expedition, go heavily armed in broad daylight, and take the group forcibly from anyone who got in the way." The real trouble was likely to happen once they got the runaways over to Ohio, where there was a reward of $1,000 for the recapture of the fugitive slaves. Slave catchers or reward-seeking townspeople would be watching.

Luckily, common sense convinced the expedition to wait until dark. That night Parker and the Rankins took three boats across the Ohio River to the Kentucky shore. They found the hiding fugitives "all right, scared and hungry." Once they and the rescued fugitives landed in Ripley, they were joined by abolitionists who had met with the Rankins and Parker earlier that morning. The well-armed group marched with the fugitives straight through the middle of Ripley "to the Rankin house, without being disturbed by the town or attacked by the law," recounted Parker. After a meal prepared by Mrs. Rankin, the fugitives were shuttled to a safer station and put on the Underground Railroad to Canada.

Thus have I been attacked at midnight with fire and weapons of death, and nothing but the good providence of God has preserved my property from flames and myself and family from violence and death. And why? Have I wronged any one? No, but I am an ABOLITIONIST. I do not recognize the slaveholder's right to the flesh and blood and souls of men and women. For this I must be proscribed, my property burnt, and my life put in jeopardy! Now I desire all men to know that I am not to be deterred from what I believe to be my duty by fire and sword. I also wish all to know that I feel it my duty to defend my HOME to the very uttermost, and that it is as much as duty to shoot the midnight assassin in his attacks as it is to pray.

REVEREND JOHN RANKIN, an Underground Railroad stationmaster

Another Underground Railroad partnership that helped thousands of fugitive slaves escape to freedom was less violent—but no less exciting. Thomas Garrett was a Quaker, a coal and iron merchant, an abolitionist, and an Underground Railroad stationmaster who lived in Wilmington, Delaware (see page 89). Because Delaware was a slave state, Garrett's work helping slaves was especially risky. Garrett often sent fugitives from Wilmington on to Philadelphia, in the free state of Pennsylvania, only 30

miles (48 kilometers) away. Garrett soon developed a partnership with a young man named William Still (see page 79), who worked in the Pennsylvania Anti-Slavery Society office. Still was part of Philadelphia's large free black community. He, too, was a stationmaster. Still and his wife hid fugitives passing through Philadelphia. In addition, William Still was something truly rare in the Underground Railroad. He was a record keeper.

RUNAWAY SLAVES FLEEING KENTUCKY AND WEST VIRGINIA HAD TO CROSS THE OHIO RIVER TO ENTER THE FREE STATE OF OHIO.

Still wrote down the names of the fugitives that came through his office. He also wrote down their stories, asking many why they chose to risk escape. Still even kept records of money given by the society to conductors such as Harriet Tubman, and of the shoes, train tickets, and food that money was used to buy. Still also kept the letters that Garret sent him about fugitives heading his way. Many mostly white antislavery groups raised money for mostly black vigilance committees to help fugitives. But it was very unusual for blacks and whites to directly work together in the 1800s. Even cities in free states, such as Philadelphia, Pennsylvania, were divided by race. There were separate stores, churches, funeral homes, schools, and even streetcars for black and white people. William Still's and Thomas Garrett's partnership—and friendship—was a fortunate exception.

◈◈ *[Our Underground Railroad agent, Mr. Rice] took us to where there were a great many freight cars, and then producing a large key and looking hastily around to see we were not noticed, he opened quickly the slide on a caboose car and had us climb in, then getting in with us he securely bolted the car on the inside, while another man friendly to us locked it outside. He went with the train, and kept a kind of watchful care of this particular car . . . At last we reached Philadelphia, and Mr. Rice took us through the crowded streets up to the underground railroad office and introduced us to the chief man, Mr. William S[t]ill. He was very kind, indeed, and took an especial interest in our case, listening attentively while we told him the main incidents of our lives.*

▨ Isaac D. Williams, a former Virginia slave who escaped to Canada

SLAVE CATCHERS OFTEN HAD ARMED ENCOUNTERS WITH FLEEING RUNAWAYS AND UNDERGROUND RAILROAD WORKERS.

As a slave in Delaware, Ann Maria Jackson had heard the name Thomas Garrett. She was married to a free black man who had recently "died in the poor-house, a raving maniac," having gone insane after their two eldest children were sold away to a Mississippi plantation. All children born to slave mothers were automatically enslaved—even if their fathers were free. "It almost broke my heart," Jackson told Still, "when he came and took my children away as soon as they were big enough to hand me a drink of water." She decided that no one would ever take away any of her other children. In the chill of November, she fled with her seven remaining children. Free blacks hid the family as they journeyed north.

As the fugitive family neared Wilmington, Garrett was told that they were coming. "We had some trouble," Garrett later wrote in a letter to Still, "as they could not travel far on foot, and could not safely cross any of the bridges on the canal, either on foot or in carriage." The bridges spanning the canals south of Wilmington were being watched by slave catchers. Garret quickly sent a man with a carriage to find them. "But owing to spies they did not reach him till 10 o'clock this morning in a second carriage . . . I think they are all safe . . . If you see them they can tell their own tales." Still did meet Ann Maria Jackson, and he wrote down her tale. Then he sent Ann Maria, Mary Ann,

WILLIAM STILL

(1821–1902)

WILLIAM STILL was born a free black in New Jersey. His mother, Charity Still, was a fugitive slave who'd escaped—twice—from Maryland. The second time she escaped she changed her name to avoid being tracked down again. Young William Still helped his father run their farm, and he had little time for schooling. But he studied on his own as much as he could. At age 20 he left home and moved to Philadelphia, Pennsylvania, to find work. Still eventually landed a job as a clerk at the Pennsylvania Anti-Slavery Society. Philadelphia was a major stop on the eastern route of the Underground Railroad. Still and his wife, Letitia, soon became stationmasters, and they sheltered many runaways in their home. When Philadelphia formed a vigilance committee, Still served as its chairman. William Still had become a leader in Philadelphia's abolitionist and free black communities.

William Still took it upon himself to interview the runaways he helped. He wanted to hear about their courageous journeys and struggles. One day a former slave named Peter Friedman came into Still's office looking for information. The man explained to Still that he'd been left in the care of relatives as a child when his slave mother escaped to the North. Friedman thought that he might have family nearby. As Still listened to Friedman's story, it sounded more and more familiar. Unbelievably, Peter Friedman was William Still's long-lost brother! The happy reunion between Still's brother and their mother inspired Still to begin writing down the histories of escaped slaves. William Still later published the stories in a popular book called *The Underground Railroad.*

THOMAS GARRETT.

William Henry, Frances Sabrina, Wilhelmina, John Edwin, Ebenezer Thomas, and William Albert Jackson along on the Underground Railroad. They all arrived in Canada safely. These eight fugitives were among thousands that Garrett and Still helped to freedom.

Treacherous Travel

Like many slaves, William didn't have a last name. Born a slave in Kentucky and moved to Missouri, William knew the horrors of slavery (see page 82). He'd seen his mother whipped, been forced to trim the gray hairs from slaves' whiskers in preparation for their auction, and had his own family sold away from him. William had tried to escape several times. The first time, he was quickly caught by slave-hunting bloodhounds. Another time he escaped with his mother. They'd walked for 10 days before slave hunters caught them. William was finally able to escape while working as a hired-out slave on a steamboat traveling the Ohio River. When the steamboat docked on the Ohio shore, William jumped ship.

I found that it would be impossible to carry anything with me but what was upon my person. I had some provisions, and a single suit of clothes, about half worn. [From the steamboat] I made directly for the woods, where I remained until night, knowing well that I could not travel, even in the state of Ohio, during the day, without danger of being arrested . . . After dark, I emerged from the woods into a narrow path, which led me into the main travelled road. But I knew not which way to go. I did not know north from south, east from west. I looked in vain for the North Star; a heavy cloud hid it from my view. I walked up and down the road until near midnight, when the clouds disappeared, and I welcomed the sight of my friend—truly the slave's friend—the North Star! As soon as I saw it, I knew my course, and

PETER STILL (LEFT), THE BROTHER OF WILLIAM STILL, AND THEIR MOTHER, CHARITY STILL (RIGHT).

before daylight I travelled twenty or twenty-five miles. It being in the winter, I suffered intensely from the cold; being without an overcoat, and my other clothes rather thin for the season. . . . I travelled at night, and lay by during the day. . . . On the fourth day my provisions gave out . . . I went to a barn on the road-side and there found some ears of corn. I took ten or twelve of them, and kept on my journey. . . . On the fifth or six day, it rained very fast, and froze about as fast as it fell, so that my clothes were one glare of ice. I travelled on at night until I became so chilled and benumbed— the wind blowing into my face—that I found it impossible to go any further, and accordingly took shelter in a barn, where I was obliged to walk about to keep from freezing. Nothing but the providence of God, and that old barn, saved me from freezing to death. I received a very severe cold, which settled upon my lungs, and from time to time my feet had been frost-bitten, so that it was with difficulty I could walk. In this situation I travelled two days, when I found that I must seek shelter somewhere, or die.

⊞ WILLIAM WELLS BROWN, an abolitionist, Underground Railroad stationmaster, and former slave

A kind man named Wells Brown sheltered William for two weeks while the runaway regained his strength and his frostbitten feet healed. William was so grateful to his rescuer

NAVIGATE BY THE NORTH STAR

MANY ESCAPING SLAVES trying to reach freedom in the North used the North Star to guide them. The North Star, or Polaris, doesn't move across the sky or change place from season to season, as other stars do. Polaris never changes position—it always points to the north.

The stars that make up the "pouring edge" of the easy-to-locate Big Dipper point to the North Star. Here's how you can spot the North Star yourself.

1. Find the Big Dipper, or Drinking Gourd. It's a group of seven bright stars in the northern or northwest sky that form the shape of a ladle with a curved handle.

2. Look at the bowl part of the Big Dipper. The side of the bowl further from the handle is the "pouring edge." The two stars that make up the pouring edge of the Big Dipper point toward the North Star. Just follow the bottom pouring-edge star to the top one and keep going!

that he took his name as his own last name. He crossed Ohio to Lake Erie and eventually made his way to Canada. William Wells Brown knew firsthand the dangers and hardships endured on the journey to freedom. He wrote that "Nothing but the prospect of enjoying liberty could have induced me to undergo such trials, for 'Behind I left the whips and chains, Before me were sweet Freedom's plains!' This, and this alone, cheered me onward."

Brown's story reveals hardships that were often encountered by runaways. Simply knowing which road to take or stream to follow was sometimes impossible. Many, like Brown, followed the North Star. Slaves learned how to find the unmoving star by hearing songs like

$100 REWARD —

Ran away the subscriber, living on Herring Bay, Anne Arundel Co., Md., on Saturday, 28th January, Negro man Elijah, who calls himself Elijah Cook; is about 21 years of age, well made, of a very dark complexion, has an impediment in his speech, and a scar on his left cheek bone, apparently occasioned by a shot.

—J. SCRIVENER

FROM THE ANNAPOLIS, MARYLAND, *REPUBLIC,* FEBRUARY 1837.

HERO OF FREEDOM
WILLIAM WELLS BROWN
(C.1814–1884)

WILLIAM WELLS BROWN was born a slave in Kentucky. After several tries, he finally escaped to Canada at about age 20. After escaping, Brown immediately started helping other slaves out of bondage. He moved to Buffalo, New York, which is very close to the Canadian border. His home became an important Underground Railroad station. Brown also became an abolitionist. He spoke at meetings and gave lectures about the horrors of slavery he'd seen and experienced. During the 1850s he gave more than 1,000 antislavery speeches in Europe alone. During the Civil War, William Wells Brown helped recruit African Americans to fight for the Union army and end slavery.

William Wells Brown never went to school. It was illegal for slaves to learn to read or write. Once he was free, Brown worked hard to educate himself. He wrote his first book in 1847. It is called *Narrative of William W. Brown: A Fugitive Slave, Written by Himself.* The book was very popular, and Brown went on to become a successful author. He wrote books about many topics, including abolitionism, history, and travel. William Wells Brown was also the first African American novelist. His novel is called *Clotel, or the President's Daughter.*

"Following the Drinking Gourd." ("Drinking Gourd" is another name for the Big Dipper star grouping.) But on cloudy nights, fugitives might have to guess which way was north by looking for moss on trees, which usually grows on the cooler north side of their trunks. But it was still very easy to lose one's way running through woods and fields. Getting lost added more difficult days to the already lengthy journey of runaways.

Most runaway slaves fled their masters empty-handed. Finding food along their way was a struggle, and many went hungry. Harsh weather was another problem, as few slaves owned heavy winter clothing, and shelter was often scarce. Many slaves chose to escape in the spring so they'd have all summer to get to Canada before winter came. Others slaves waited until there was corn in the fields to provide food along the way. Many runaways crossed into free states and reached the Underground Railroad sick, exhausted, frostbitten, and half starved.

FOLLOW THE DRINKING GOURD

SLAVES LEARNED how to find and follow the North Star by hearing songs such as "Follow the Drinking Gourd." "Drinking Gourd" is another name for the Big Dipper, the group of stars that points to the North Star (see page 81).

Follow the music and verses below to sing the famous song yourself. Refer to the Underground Railroad code phrases found on page 54 to better understand the song's message.

"Follow the Drinking Gourd"

CHORUS:
Follow the Drinking Gourd! Follow the Drinking Gourd.
For the old man is awaiting to carry you to freedom,
If you follow the Drinking Gourd.

FIRST VERSE:
When the sun comes back and the first quail calls,
Follow the Drinking Gourd.
For the old man is waiting for to carry you to freedom,
If you follow the Drinking Gourd.

(chorus)

SECOND VERSE:
The river bank makes a very good road,
The dead trees show you the way,
Left foot, peg foot, traveling on
Follow the Drinking Gourd.

(chorus)

THIRD VERSE:
The river ends between two hills,
Follow the Drinking Gourd.
There's another river on the other side,
Follow the Drinking Gourd.

(chorus)

FOURTH VERSE:
Where the great big river meets the little river,
Follow the Drinking Gourd.
For the old man is awaiting to carry you to freedom,
If you follow the Drinking Gourd.

CHAPTER 4

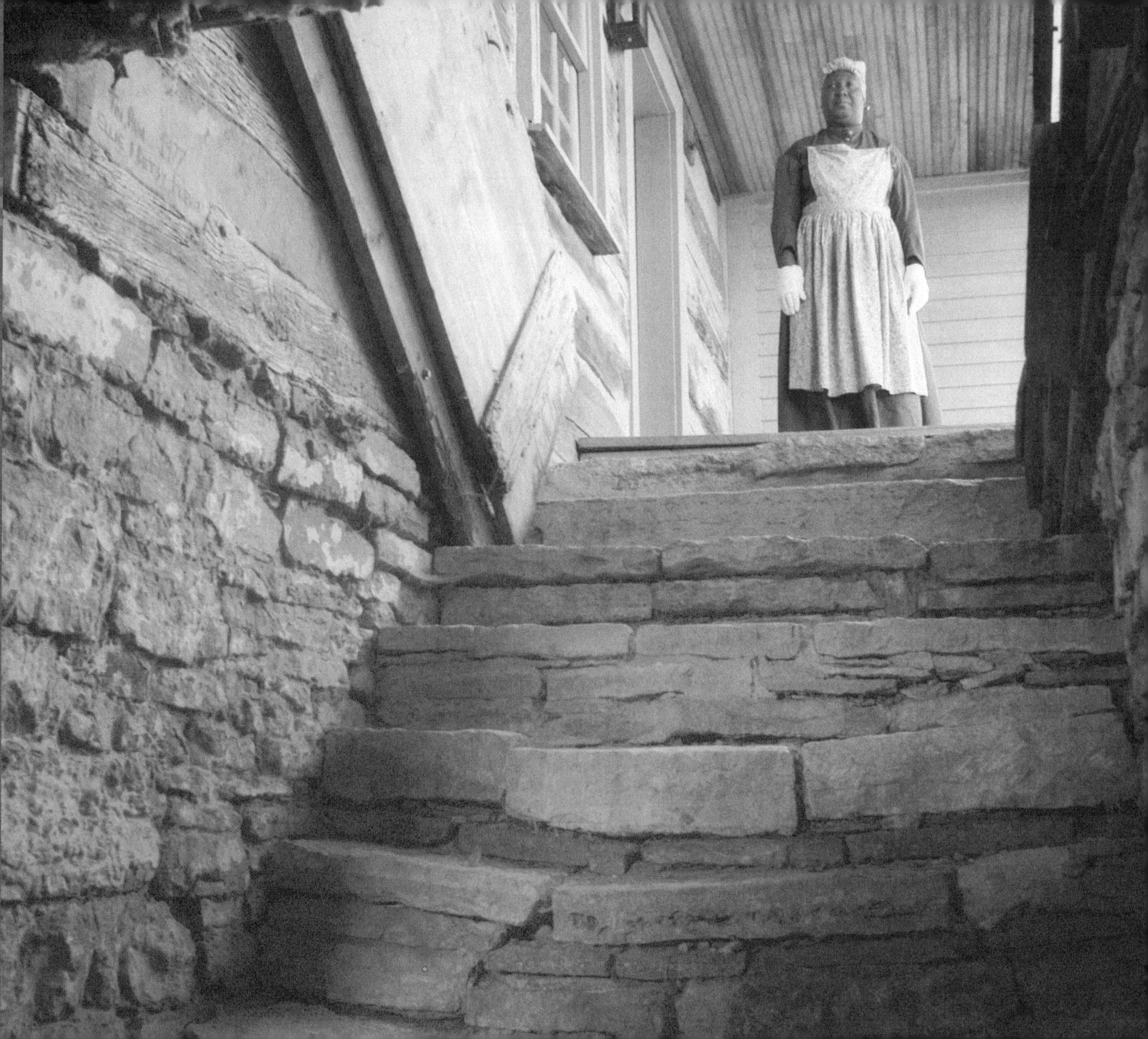

Stationmasters

*Hiding Passengers
from Slave Catchers*

MANY DANGERS faced Harriet Tubman and her passengers as they fled north. The borders between slave states and free states were flooded with slave hunters, bloodhounds, and lawmen. Conductor Tubman traveled with weapons, including a revolver, and she was willing to do whatever it took to make her missions successful. Sometimes that meant threatening a wavering runaway! When an exhausted, frightened fugitive slave wanted to give up and go back to the plantation, Tubman was known to pull out her gun. Dead men tell no tales, Harriet reminded the runaway: "You go on or die!" She wasn't going to risk her precious "cargo" with possible betrayal by a runaway who'd changed his or her mind.

As she made more daring trips into the South, Harriet's fame grew. She was called Moses, because, like the biblical figure, she delivered her people from slavery and seemed untouchable by her enemies. Wherever she showed up in the South, slaves wanting to escape asked her to guide them to freedom. Former slaves in the North sought Harriet out to ask her to rescue their family members who had been left behind in bondage.

Slave owners were outraged by Harriet's missions into the South. The rewards offered for her capture eventually amounted to the equivalent of more than $850,000 in today's money! Once, while traveling north on a train, a person who was sitting beside Harriet suddenly said her name. Had someone recognized her? As she hid her face under her big hat, Harriet realized that the person was reading a runaway slave poster about her out loud! Harriet got off at the next station and took a train headed south. Who'd look for a fugitive slave traveling south toward slavery?

Harriet avoided capture by disguising herself, too. No one looking for a black woman gave Harriet a second look when she was dressed as a man or a crippled old woman. "There's two things I've got a right to, and these are, Death or Liberty—one or the other I mean to have," said Harriet. "No one will take me back alive; I shall fight for my liberty, and when the time has come for me to go, the Lord will let them kill me."

At first, Harriet just conducted her passengers to the free states of the North. But the Fugitive Slave Law of 1850 changed that. It meant that fugitive slaves were no longer safe in free states. "I wouldn't trust Uncle Sam with my people no longer," explained Harriet. "I brought 'em all clear off to Canada." Getting all the way to Canada often tripled the distance that had to be traveled

by runaways—as well as the food and expenses needed. Harriet quickly stepped up her use of Underground Railroad stations. She also got help from antislavery and vigilance committee groups. When Harriet rescued her brother James Ross, his wife, and nine others in late 1851, they stopped at Frederick Douglass's station in Rochester, New York. He sheltered the group and took up a collection to help pay their expenses along their journey. Then Harriet led the 11 fugitives all the way to Canada. It was now the best way to truly be free.

Dangers on the Railroad

Once they received help from Underground Railroad conductors and stationmasters, runaways were less likely to starve, get lost, or freeze to death. But their journey became no less hazardous. Runaways were just as likely—if not more likely—to be recaptured in free states as they were in slave states. In the South, runaway slaves had to worry about their owners coming after them as well as being captured by local lawmen or slave patrols. Slave patrols captured and jailed all slaves found more than a few miles from their home. There were no slave patrols in the free states of the North. But runaways still had to look out for local lawmen in the North, as well as for their prowling owners. Many areas in free states were proslavery and had activist groups that were happy to recapture slaves for Southern owners. The Knights of the Gold Circle, for example, was a proslavery group in southwestern Ohio that worked to keep runaway slaves from running through their area.

❁ *[The stationmaster] accompanied me on my way toward Columbus [Ohio] till break of day . . . and bid me God-speed. In less than an hour after I left him, I passed a place where several men were out early . . . One cried out "ha! there, have you got any pass? where are you going?" I told them it was none of their business. They attempted to stop me, but I ran from them into the woods . . . I rambled through the woods all that day and the ensuing night in search of the road I had left. I found the road next morning, but was . . . faint and hungry, having lost my provisions in the chase . . . I enquired of a man who was splitting wood in a yard, for a road called Whetstone, which leads to Upper Sandusky [on Lake Erie]. He raised the stick he was splitting and attempted to knock me down; but I was too quick for him—wielded my old hoe handle and with one blow brought him to the ground. I then escaped into a cornfield . . .*

After being hunted for hours in the field like a beast, I at length succeeded in creeping through the fence undiscovered, and by crawling some distance upon the ground I gained the woods and ran till I found a good place . . . and hid.

▦ DAVID BARRETT, a former slave who escaped from Kentucky to Canada

The greatest threat to fugitive slaves came from slave catchers and slave hunters. Anyone anywhere might be tempted to turn in a runaway for reward money. But slave catchers made their living finding, hunting down, and recapturing runaways for reward money or to sell to slave traders. They were professional bounty hunters who studied the local advertisements for runaway slaves. They knew the reward amounts and were usually well armed. Slave catchers wanted to capture fugitive slaves alive so they could turn them in for a reward. But they'd often shoot them with small, spraying bullets called birdshot. One runaway was caught in North Carolina wearing a coat stuffed with turkey feathers to protect himself from birdshot. It was like a homemade bulletproof vest.

Many slave catchers owned and used special slave-hunting bloodhounds. These dogs were bred to find and follow the scent of runaways. They barked and howled when they found their prey. Runaways who were traveling on foot

ELLEN CRAFT (LEFT) AND WILLIAM CRAFT (RIGHT) ESCAPED SLAVERY BY DISGUISING THEMSELVES AS AN ILL PLANTATION OWNER AND HIS SLAVE.

[M]y master offered $2,000 reward for our recovery, and a big search was made for us. We stayed there [in Cincinnati, Ohio,] several days in hiding, and my wife said she had seen several men on horseback passing the house whom she knew to be negro traders who were trying to find us. It was a curious thing to have to go to Pittsburg [Pennsylvania] and come back so near where my wife's master lived [in Kentucky] that we could see it across the river from our hiding place. But it was well planned, and put our pursuers on a false scent. Then the arrangements were made for our departure to Canada . . . [M]yself, my wife, and two children rode away in a one horse wagon, with a load of straw on top, and so fixed that we could lie on the bottom and have enough air to breathe. We traveled at night only, and slept in barns in day time.

ALLEN SIDNEY, a former slave who escaped to Canada

tried to fool the bloodhounds by rubbing their shoes and feet with smelly onion, cow dung, or tree sap to cover the scent of their footsteps. They also waded through streams and swamps to throw the dogs off their trail. Underground Railroad passengers, conductors, stationmasters, and agents could never be too careful. Underground Railroad routes were constantly changed to keep bounty hunters and others from learning about them. Conductors sometimes took their "cargo" on zigzagging or goose-chasing routes between stations to throw slave catchers off their trail.

Wagons, equipped with false bottoms or filled with straw, were commonly used to hide traveling fugitives. Another way that runaways avoided capture was by disguising themselves. If slave catchers were looking for a young male runaway, dressing him up as an old woman could save him from being recognized. Likewise, a group of fugitives dressed as workers and carrying tools were much more likely to make it across a bridge without being questioned. Runaway slave advertisements often gave descriptions of a fugitive's skin color, hair color and style, and clothes. A runaway slave girl advertised as "light-skinned with long hair" could easily be missed by slave catchers if she was dressed in boys' clothes, her hair was cut, and her skin was darkened with burnt cork.

William and Ellen Craft were slaves in the Deep South state of Georgia. They knew they would have to make a long journey without help to reach the free states. To help ensure their success, the Crafts decided to try something quite daring. Ellen Craft pretended to be a young white man. She dressed in a suit and boots, cut her hair short, and wore tinted glasses. She was light-skinned as it was, and she covered up much of her beardless face with a large bandage. Her husband played the part of a house slave. The Crafts told people that they were an ill young man traveling with his servant to see a famous doctor in Philadelphia. It was a long trip for the Crafts, and they had a few close calls. But the resourceful couple made it safely to freedom.

The Underground Railroad stationmaster Thomas Garrett once helped a fugitive leave his carefully watched home undetected by dressing her as a Quaker woman wearing a large bonnet that hid her face. Many stationmasters kept disguises on hand for fugitives. They were sometimes crafted by sewing circles of abolitionist women. But fugitives weren't the only ones to disguise themselves. Many conductors posed as people they were not, as well. Harriet Tubman was a master of disguise. On many occasions, she avoided capture by pretending to be a crippled old woman. What slave catcher could consider such a helpless creature a threat, or even worth kidnapping?

HERO OF FREEDOM

THOMAS GARRETT

(1789–1871)

THOMAS GARRETT (see page 80) was a second-generation Underground Railroad stationmaster. Garrett's Quaker parents hid runaways in their Pennsylvania farmhouse when Thomas Garrett was a boy. When a free black woman who worked for his family was kidnapped by slave traders, young Garrett ran down the kidnappers and rescued her. Garrett later said that during the daring rescue he'd had a vision in which God revealed the evil of slavery to him. The experience convinced Garrett that his life's work was to help slaves escape and end slavery.

Garrett married and soon moved to Wilmington, Delaware. There he became a wealthy iron merchant—and a famous Underground Railroad stationmaster. Living in Wilmington put Garrett on a major route that was used by slaves fleeing up the East Coast. Wilmington, in the slave state of Delaware, was the last stop before the free state of Pennsylvania. Garrett is credited with helping some 2,700 fugitives. He worked with many conductors, including Harriet Tubman, and he had a unique partnership with William Still of Philadelphia (see page 79). Garrett had many enemies among lawmen and slave owners, but African Americans protected Garrett's home from proslavery rioters during the Civil War. After the war, Garrett worked to secure the right of African Americans to vote.

15-YEAR-OLD MARIA WEEMS WAS DRESSED AS A BOY AND RENAMED JOE WRIGHT BEFORE BEING SHUTTLED ALONG THE UNDERGROUND RAILROAD.

In the morning the servant girl came down into the cellar [where I was hiding], and when I saw she was black I thought it would be best to make myself known to her, which I did, and she told me I had better remain where I was and keep quiet, and she would go and tell Mr. Nickins, one of the agents of the underground Railway. She brought me down a bowl of coffee and some bread and meat, which I relished very much, and that night she opened the cellar door gently, and called to me to come out, and introduced me to Mr. Nickins and two others, who took me to a house in Sixth street, where I remained until the next night, when they dressed me in female's clothes, and I was taken to the railway depot in a carriage—was put in the car, and sent to Cleveland, Ohio where I was placed on board a steam boat . . . and carried down Lake Erie to the city of Buffalo, New York, and the next day placed on the [train] car . . . Three hours after starting I was in Toronto, Upper Canada, where I lived for three years and sang my song of deliverance.

JACOB D. GREEN, a former slave who escaped from Kentucky

Traps and Snares

Every night of the year saw runaways, singly or in groups, making their way stealthily to the country north. Traps and snares were set for them, into which they fell by the hundreds and were returned to their homes . . . You can imagine this game of hide-and-go-seek was not without its excitements and tragedies . . . Every precaution was taken to prevent the fugitive from successfully passing through this forbidden land. The woods were patrolled nightly by constables, and any man black or white had to give a good account of himself, especially if he were a stranger. Every ford was watched, while along the creeks and the [Ohio] river, the skiffs were not only pulled up on shore, but were padlocked to trees, and the oars removed. There were dogs in every dooryard, ready to run down the unfortunates. Once word came from further south that runaways were on the way, the whole countryside turned out, not only to stop the fugitives, but to claim the reward for their capture. Everything was organized against the slaves' getaway.

JOHN PARKER, an Underground Railroad conductor and former slave

Fugitive slaves who were running north couldn't be too careful. Slave patrols, lawmen, and bounty hunters weren't the only ones out to get them. There were also proslavery spies and greedy con artists who pretended to be abolitionists or Underground Railroad workers. They'd approach runaways, gain their trust, and then betray them for the reward. Many runaways were so wary of betrayal that they neither sought nor accepted any help—from blacks or whites—while fleeing. The schemes were endless. One band of crooks kidnapped free blacks and took them into the South. Then they printed up runaway slave advertisements that included the descriptions of those they'd kidnapped. They used the ads as "proof" in court that the kidnapped free blacks were slaves, whom they owned! The unfortunate people were then sold away to slavery—often in the Deep South.

Lewis Williams was a Kentucky slave who had escaped slavery as a boy and lived as a free black in Cincinnati, Ohio. As a young man, he fell in love, and he wondered if the young woman loved him as well. Williams decided to ask a fortune-teller. The fortune-teller asked Williams where he was born, and during the conversation she realized that he was a fugitive slave. The fortune-teller got Williams to give her the name of his former master, too. When Williams left, she contacted his former owner. The slave owner promised to pay the fortune-teller $200 if she'd tell him where Lewis Williams could be found. She did, and marshals soon arrested him. Fortunately, free blacks in Cincinnati were able to rescue him from the courtroom, and Williams was quickly put on the Underground Railroad to Canada.

GET LOST IN DISGUISE

RUNAWAY SLAVE ADS and slave catchers used physical descriptions of fugitive slaves to help identify them. Many runaways were able to avoid capture by using disguises that changed their appearances. If slave catchers were looking for a young female runaway, dressing up as an old man could save her from being recognized. Many Underground Railroad workers, including Harriet Tubman, were also known to disguise themselves.

YOU'LL NEED
- ☒ Mirror
- ☒ Pen or pencil
- ☒ Paper
- ☒ Clothes that you don't normally wear
- ☒ Eyeglasses, wigs, hats, or other accessories to disguise yourself
- ☒ Costume makeup (optional)
- ☒ Spray-on nonpermanent hair dye (optional)

1. Imagine that someone was printing up a "wanted" poster of you, or a runaway slave ad about you. How would they describe you? Look at yourself in a mirror, and then write up a description of yourself. Include how old you are, whether you're a boy or a girl, and your hair color, skin color, height, weight, and so forth.

2. Look at yourself in the mirror again. Read the description you wrote. Think about how you could change how you look so that the description would no longer fit.

3. Disguise yourself! Dress in different clothing, wear sunglasses, or do whatever you can to disguise yourself.

BROUGHT TO JAIL — In Irwinton, Wilkinson County, (Ga.) 16th Nov. 1837, a negro man by the name of **JACOB**, who says he belongs to Heritan Middleton, in Henry County, Alabama. He says he was hired to John Webb, near West Point, in this State. He is about 6 feet high, dark complexion, and slow in speaking. There are no marks discoverable, only he is very badly shot in the right side and right hand. The owner or owners are requested to come forward, prove property, pay charges, and take him away.

—S. B. MURPHEY, Jailer

FROM THE *GEORGIA JOURNAL*, JANUARY 2, 1838.

It was nightfall when, tired, worn and footsore, I entered the streets of the town. I was just faint with exhaustion and could hardly drag myself along . . . [A] quiet, decent looking man whom I met . . . then said, 'I know who you are; don't be alarmed. I'm a friend to such as you and will help all the slaves I can to escape.' He talked so cheerfully and gave me such kindly counsel that a great load seemed to lift from my mind and I felt hope arise anew in my breast . . . I now entered an office in the lower end of the town where my conductor said he had some business. The moment we got into a little room, where there were a lot of rough men sitting around, he said, 'Well, boys, I've brought you a runaway nigger I've captured. Lock him up while we look for his owner.' They led me away and put me in a cell, for it was a police station to which I had been decoyed, and it seems there was an advertisement in one of the city papers, describing me and offering a reward for my capture.

⊠ HENRY BANKS, a former slave who, after many attempts, escaped to Canada

One of the most famous criminal slave catchers was Patty Cannon. She and her "Johnson Gang" sold off kidnapped free blacks and captured fugitives into the Deep South. Runaways and kidnapped free blacks were chained up in the basement, attic, and nearby woods surrounding her home on the Maryland–Delaware border. Cannon was a large, powerful, ruthless woman. She and her gang were known for torture and murder. Cannon even paid people to pose as stationmasters and turn over fugitives resting at their fake safe houses. Cannon was finally arrested for the murder of four fugitive slaves in 1829. Before her trial, she killed herself by ingesting poison. Minerva Blockson, a descendant of slaves who once lived near Cannon's home, recounted how adults would tease children by telling them "how evil old Patty Canon would catch us and sell us to slavers down south."

Fighting Back

Proslavers and criminals weren't the only ones using violence and deception. Some Underground Railroad workers posed as anti-abolitionists in order to spy on proslavery groups. What better way to know what they were up to? And, as the stories that emerged from Ripley, Ohio, point out, there was bloodshed on both sides. Slaves in search of freedom were also willing to fight.

The slaves are watched by patrols, who ride about to try to catch them off the [slave] quarters, especially at the house of a free person of color. I

have known the slaves to stretch clothes line across the street, high enough to let the horse pass, but not the rider; then the boys would run, and the patrols in full chase would be thrown off by running against the line. The patrols are poor white men, who live by plundering and stealing, getting rewards for runaways.

⊠ Francis Henderson, a former slave who escaped from Washington, D.C., to Canada

On Christmas Eve in 1855, six slaves decided to take advantage of their master's holiday celebration. The fleeing slaves took their owner's carriage and horses and escaped. They knew it would be a long, hard journey to Canada in the dead of winter. But the group was determined not to be recaptured—and they armed themselves with guns and knives to make sure of it. The cold and snow made travel slow for the fugitives, four of whom rode in the carriage, while the other two rode on horseback. But hunger and frostbite was soon to be the least of their worries.

While crossing the slave state of Maryland, six white men and a boy approached the runaways. The men suspected that they were fugitives and demanded that they surrender. Knowing that if they surrendered they'd be taken back to slavery, the runaways pulled out their weapons. The white men let them go on

WHEN A GROUP OF MEN STOPPED THESE RUNAWAYS ON CHRISTMAS EVE, THE FUGITIVES PULLED OUT THEIR WEAPONS.

their way. Later, unfortunately, two of the runaways, who were on horseback, became separated from those in the carriage and were captured. The other four—Barnaby and Mary Elizabeth Grigby, Frank Wanzer, and Emily Foster—arrived in Philadelphia frostbitten but alive. After being nursed back to health by the city's vigilance committee, the four told their story to William Still. All four runaways eventually reached Canada via the Underground Railroad. But Frank Wanzer left

DESIGN A HIDING PLACE

SOME STATIONMASTERS went to great lengths to hide fugitive slaves from lawmen and slave catchers. Hidden trap doors that led to secret rooms or escape tunnels were sometimes installed in Underground Railroad stations, or safe houses. Some stations had closets or rooms with extra walls that created temporary hiding places for fugitives. You can design a hiding place for your own home in this activity.

YOU'LL NEED
- Paper
- Pencil

YOU MAY NEED
- Box
- Glue
- Cardboard
- Styrofoam
- Construction paper
- Balsa wood
- Paint
- Scissors
- Tape
- Clay

1. If you were an Underground Railroad stationmaster and your home was a station, where would you hide your passengers? Here are a few ideas:

- *Is there a crawl space beneath the first floor of your house? Create a trapdoor under a rug and hide runaways under the floor.*

- *Is there a space under a stairway, at the back of a big closet, in an attic, or in the basement? Create a hidden room by adding a fake wall with a small doorway. Don't forget to hide the doorway with a poster, painting, or piece of furniture!*

- *Is there somewhere safe nearby that runaways could escape to? Design an escape tunnel that leads from your house to a barn, shed, park, church, or other safe place.*

- *Do you live in an apartment or two-family home? Design an escape route from your home to a helpful neighbors' home*

2. Decide what sort of hiding place would work best for your home, and draw your detailed design on paper.

3. Decide the best way to build a three-dimensional model, or diorama, of your design—and then build it! You can lay an open box on its side and build the model inside it. Or your diorama can be freestanding. You can create the model using balsa wood, cardboard, construction paper, pieces of Styrofoam, or clay.

Canada a year later. He bravely returned to Virginia to successfully conduct his still-enslaved relatives to freedom.

Safe Havens

On I went from one station to another, everywhere being received and lodged as though I were a chosen guest. Even if it was after midnight, all in the house, from the aged grandmother to the little children, would get up and crowd around me, listening to my sorrows and shedding alternately tears of joy and grief at my escape, and the pangs I endured. How shall I, who up to my forty-sixth year was an illiterate slave, find words wherein to express my eternal gratitude, to those who so kindly assisted me.

REV. FRANCIS FREDERICK, a former slave who escaped from Virginia to Canada

Underground Railroad safe houses, called stations, were havens for fugitives who were on the run. They were places where a fugitive could find a rare day's rest and often a meal. But finding safe stations wasn't always easy. There were no telephones back then. The only way to know where a station was and whether it was safe was by written message or word of mouth. Most runaways—and many Underground Railroad workers—couldn't read. And being caught with a letter, even one that was written using Underground Railroad code words, might get a stationmaster arrested. Fugitives who traveled with the help of Underground Railroad conductors and agents were often given names or descriptions of stations and told to memorize the information. But it was up often up the runaways to find that station and figure out if it was safe to approach it. There was always the possibility of being watched. Some fugitives were instructed to make a bird call, use a special knock, or ask for a particular person as a way to identify themselves as passengers on the Underground Railroad. Many simply borrowed the Quaker introduction of "I'm a friend with friends." But knocking on a station door was always risky.

THIS PAINTING SHOWS UNDERGROUND RAILROAD WORKERS, INCLUDING STATIONMASTERS LEVI AND CATHERINE COFFIN, HELPING ARRIVING FUGITIVES.

I observed, on casting my eyes over the town, a woman standing outside her home, close beside a rain barrel. I said: "Boys, that is a colored woman; let us go and speak to her."... What was our surprise and joy on meeting the woman to find we had come directly to the very house, that was one of the stations of the underground railway... This saved us from running into any danger we might otherwise have got into through asking questions. The lady gave us food, made a bed for us on the floor, and kept us all night. She said...

one of the agents of the underground road... would see to our next move.

ISAAC D. WILLIAMS, a former Virginia slave who escaped to Canada

I had been instructed by my friend to seek out a certain coloured man, on my arrival at the town in which I now was, and where there was a considerable settlement of Quakers... My new friend was at home, and on my making myself known to him, which I did by mentioning the

name of our mutual acquaintance, he knew what I wanted. He then gave me directions to go to a certain house, which he pointed out to me, where I should be in safety. He could not accompany me, as that would have been imprudent, and have exposed him to danger. I made straight for the place, and, on being seen, was instantly taken in.

▣ JOHN BROWN, a former Georgia slave who escaped on the Underground Railroad

HERO OF FREEDOM

WILLIAM LAMBERT

(C. 1817–1890)

WILLIAM LAMBERT was born a free black in New Jersey. His father had been born a slave, but had bought his own freedom. Lambert attended school as a child and learned to read and write. While on a visit to Buffalo, New York, with a schoolmaster, Lambert got a job aboard a steamship on the Great Lakes. He eventually settled in the Great Lakes city of Detroit, Michigan. Lambert opened a tailor shop in Detroit, and he soon became a leader in the city's African American community. He helped organize the first State Convention of Colored Citizens in 1843, and he served as its chairman. Lambert encouraged blacks to fight for their freedom and equality and demand full civil rights.

Lambert was also active in the Underground Railroad. He and fellow Detroiter George De Baptiste ran a secret network called the African-American Mysteries: The Order of the Men of Oppression. The network helped thousands of runaways cross the Detroit River into Canada.

Lambert also worked to promote education for black children. After the Civil War, the successful businessman remained a leader in the community and worked for African American rights.

Many stationmasters used signals to let fugitive slaves know it was safe to approach. Some, like the Rankins, left a lamp lit in a window when no slave catchers were prowling around. Other stationmasters hung lanterns or handkerchiefs on gates and statues, put special quilts out on clotheslines, or moved a stone from one end of the porch to the other to signal slaves on the run. Runaways were often told what to look for before being conducted on to their next station.

William Lambert was a free black who moved to Detroit, Michigan, around 1838. Detroit was the last depot on the Underground Railroad for many fugitives. Windsor, Canada, is just across the Detroit River. Lambert was a successful businessman and a very successful Underground Railroad agent and stationmaster. He helped thousands—if not tens of thousands—of runaways cross the river into Canada. The secret of Lambert's success was the secrecy demanded by the agents, conductors, stationmasters, and passengers that passed through Lambert's route. They called themselves the African-American Mysteries: The Order of the Men of Oppression. This secret, mostly African American group used secret handshakes, passwords, hand signals, and test conversations to make sure no one was betrayed.

Only those fugitives and conductors who could correctly answer the following questions in a test conversation correctly—while making the secret hand signal—were passed on to stationmasters:

QUESTION: *Have you ever been on the railroad?*

ANSWER: *I have been a short distance.*

Q: *Where did you start from?*

A: *The depot.*

Q: *Where did you stop?*

A: *At a place called Safety.*

Q: *Have you a brother there? I think I know him.*

A: *I know you now. You traveled on the road.*

"This conversation was the test," William Lambert told a newspaper reporter in 1886. "It was taught to every fugitive, and the sign was pulling the knuckle of the right forefinger over the knuckle of the same finger on the left hand." Even Quakers had to use those exact words, foregoing their usual "thee" and "thou" in order to prove themselves trustworthy.

⟨⟩ *The fugitives were brought in from the country from Wayne [Indiana] and Ann Arbor [Michigan] so as to arrive at night. They would be brought to the vicinity of the lodge [in Detroit, Michigan], when we would go and test them, and all those with them . . . [W]e then took them to the rendezvous, which was the house of J.C.*

Reynolds . . . We would fetch the fugitives there, shipping them into the house by dark one by one. There they found food and warmth, and when, as frequently happened, they were ragged and thinly clad, we gave them clothing. Our boats were concealed under the docks, and before daylight we would have everyone over [the river to Canada]. We never lost a man by capture at this point, so careful were we, and we took over as high as 1,600 in one year.

⊞ WILLIAM LAMBERT, an Underground Railroad stationmaster in Detroit, Michigan

The Underground Railroad stations where runaways stayed were also sometimes very secretive. Most runaways were simply housed in barns, spare rooms, attics, basements, and cellars. But under the 1850 Fugitive Slave Law federal marshals and other lawmen accompanying slave catchers could enter and search any home, day or night, with no warning. Many stationmasters built special hiding places for fugitives in case their homes were searched by slave hunters. Some cut trap doors out of floorboards, threw a rug on top of the secret trap door, and hid runaways under foot. Others built false walls in the backs of closets or under stairways. The small doors leading behind the false walls were hidden behind a dresser or bureau. Fake wells or cisterns that never held a

SHAKE ON IT

RUNAWAY SLAVES as well as Underground Railroad stationmasters and conductors had to be careful about whom they trusted. Many slave catchers and lawmen tried to trick fugitives and Underground Railroad workers into revealing themselves. One Detroit vigilance committee that helped fugitive slaves get to Canada used secret handshakes, passwords, hand signals, and test conversations to make sure no one was betrayed.

Invent your own foolproof system of identification—a secret handshake. You can do a double or triple shake by quickly shaking hands two or three times. Or try adding finger snaps, high fives, or claps to a handshake. Sliding palms, bumping fists, touching thumbs, hooking pinkies, folding fingers, or any other unusual movement can be part of a secret handshake.

Once you've made up a unique handshake, teach it to friends or family members. Then have them test it out on each other. You can also invent a secret door-knocking pattern. Teach it to those you want to be able to identify before they enter your room!

drop of water were other clever hiding places for fugitive slaves.

Quite a few Underground Railroad stations included escape routes. Some simply had many stairways, which allowed fugitive slaves a better chance to escape capture when lawmen rode up. Other stations had escape tunnels dug underneath them. These tunnels would lead fleeing runaways away from the station being searched. Some of the tunnels even lead out to riverbanks, where fugitives boarded boats and continued on their journeys.

❖ *The old [Quaker stationmaster] laid a hand upon my shoulder, and taking my other hand in his, gave me a welcome . . . I was . . . taken to an*

MOST STATIONMASTERS HOUSED RUNAWAYS IN BARNS, ATTICS, OR CELLARS.

HERO OF FREEDOM
DAVID RUGGLES
(1810–1849)

DAVID RUGGLES was a free black born in Connecticut. He moved to New York City at age 17 and found work as a grocer. After becoming a representative for the abolitionist paper *The Emancipator*, Ruggles began writing and speaking out against slavery. He also spoke against segregation and the colonization movement, the effort to resettle free blacks in Africa. In 1834 he opened a bookstore in New York City, becoming the first African American bookseller in the country. From his store he sold antislavery books and pamphlets, printed written materials, and wrote letters for illiterate customers. Ruggles was also a self-taught physician. William Lloyd Garrison and Sojourner Truth were among his many patients.

David Ruggles headed the New York Committee of Vigilance when Frederick Douglass escaped slavery in 1838. Stationmaster Ruggles housed Douglass and helped him on to Connecticut. It's estimated that Ruggles aided as many as 1,000 runaways in New York City. He was known for fearlessly boarding ships and entering homes to find kidnapped blacks and recaptured runaways. Ruggles was also a daring legal defender of recaptured runaway slaves. He went to hearings and followed the fugitives' court cases, which angered federal magistrates. Ruggles was arrested a number of times, and he narrowly avoided being sent into slavery in the South as punishment.

upper room, where I had a good wash, in a white basin, and where clean linen and a complete suit of clothes were brought to me . . . It was the first time in my life I had found myself in such grand company . . . I was quite bewildered. "Come, friend John Brown, thee must eat," said the kind old lady, heaping my plate up with fried ham and eggs. "Thee need'nt be afraid of eating." . . . My appetite came with my courage, and then—oh! how I did eat! . . . I had not eaten a meal for so long, that now it seemed as though I never could satisfy my craving. I was then conducted into a safe retreat, where there was a comfortable bed provided for me, into which I got, and soon fell asleep . . . I felt so singularly happy, however, notwithstanding the fear I was in . . . that I was in a friend's house, and that I really was free and safe.

▨ JOHN BROWN, a former Georgia slave who escaped on the Underground Railroad

ESCAPING FUGITIVE SLAVES USED THIS TUNNEL (LEFT) UNDERNEATH THE OLD TAVERN, A HISTORIC TAVERN IN UNIONVILLE, OHIO, IN THE NORTHEAST CORNER OF THE STATE. ⊠ THIS WAS A HIDING PLACE FOR FUGITIVE SLAVES IN THE ONCE-ACTIVE UNDERGROUND RAILROAD TOWN OF SPRINGBORO, OHIO. THE LADDER (RIGHT) IS BEHIND A FALSE WALL IN A CLOSET. THE LADDER LEADS TO A TRAPDOOR THAT GOES TO THE ATTIC.

A number of towns had so many active Underground Railroad workers and safe houses that the towns themselves were like giant stations. These towns usually included large communities of free blacks and often Quakers. More than 9,000 runaways escaped to freedom via Philadelphia, Pennsylvania. Fugitives could blend in with the free black communities of places like Philadelphia and Springboro, Ohio. These towns were full of black and white Underground Railroad workers and stations.

Springboro was a Quaker town so committed to aiding runaways that a system of escape tunnels was built into many of the homes and businesses as they were constructed. Oberlin, Ohio, was another town on the Underground Railroad that was committed to helping fugitives to freedom.

Like many others in 1858, a fugitive slave named John Price was desperately trying to get to Canada. And Price was nearly there. He'd reached Oberlin, Ohio. It was only 20 more miles to the shores of Lake Erie. Canada lay just across its waters. Unfortunately, a U.S. marshal and three slave catchers were in Oberlin, too. They captured Price and took him to a hotel in nearby Wellington to wait for a train back to Kentucky—and slavery. The news of Price's capture spread like wildfire through Oberlin. Students from Oberlin College set out for Wellington on foot. Free black and white townspeople alike jumped on horses and got into their carriages. They vowed aloud that no fugitive slave would ever be taken from Oberlin. When the mob got to Wellington they surrounded the hotel where Price was being held. The rescuers stormed the hotel and carried Price out a window. They took him back to Oberlin, hid him, and eventually helped him get to Canada. Thirty-seven of the rescuers were arrested, and 20 served some time in jail. But no one was sorry that they had helped to free Price.

Unfortunately, not all escape attempts were successful. Nor were all Underground Railroad stations safe. The sad tale of Margaret Garner is proof of it. Margaret and Robert Garner were Kentucky slaves with four children. When the Ohio River froze solid in January of 1856 the family of six decided to risk escape. They fled in a horse-drawn sleigh to the river's edge, then walked across the solid ice to Cincinnati, Ohio. It was morning by the time the fleeing family made their way to Cincinnati's bustling waterfront. Local slave catchers also knew that the river was frozen. It's likely that they saw the Garners stopping to ask where the Kites lived. The Kites were free blacks and relatives of Margaret Garner. When the Garners reached the Kites' home, Elijah Kite was worried that his cousin and her family had been spotted. He hurried down to Levi Coffin's store. Maybe the famous Underground Railroad stationmaster could help get them out of town.

✧✧✧ *Kite felt alarmed for the safety of the party that had arrived at his house . . . he came to my store . . . to ask counsel regarding them. I told him that they were in a very unsafe place and must be removed at once. I directed him how to conduct them from his house to the outskirts of the city . . . to a settlement of colored people in the western part of the city, where fugitives were often harbored. I would make arrangements to forward*

HERO OF FREEDOM
— REV. JERMAIN WESLEY LOGUEN —
(C. 1813–1872)

JERMAIN WESLEY LOGUEN was born a slave in Tennessee. His first attempt to escape failed. But when his sister was sold away he decided to run away again (see pages 44–45). At age 21 he made it out of Tennessee, through Kentucky and Indiana, and to Canada via Detroit, Michigan. Once a free man in Canada, Loguen learned to read. He eventually worked in New York State, attended school, and became a minister and abolitionist speaker and writer.

Loguen and his wife settled in Syracuse, New York, and Loguen became a minister in the African Methodist Episcopal Zion Church. The Loguens' home and church soon became stations on the Underground Railroad. Loguen had a secret apartment in his home where fugitives could hide. Jermain and Caroline Loguen helped 1,500 runaways reach Canada.

Loguen was also the manager of the Fugitive Aid Society in Syracuse, and he worked to find fugitives jobs in the town's farms and businesses. Because of his efforts, Syracuse became known as "the Canada of the United States," and Loguen, the "King of the Underground Railroad."

them northward, that night, on the Underground Railroad.

⊞ LEVI COFFIN, Underground Railroad Stationmaster

But Coffin's advice came too late. The owners of the Garners and a group of lawmen surrounded the Kite home minutes after Elijah Kite returned from Coffin's store. But the Garners had no intention of surrendering. Margaret

Garner declared that she'd kill herself and her children before she'd let them be taken back to slavery. One of the lawmen broke through a window, and Robert Garner starting shooting.

As the posse overpowered her husband and stormed into the house, Margaret Garner began to carry out her threat. She grabbed a knife and slit the throat of her toddler daughter. Garner was trying to kill her other children when the slave catchers seized her. The family was captured. Some wanted Margaret arrested for murdering her daughter. But a federal court in Cincinnati ruled that the Garners be returned to their owner—they were his property under the law. The slave owner sold the "troublemaking" family down South to the owner of a cotton plantation. While traveling by boat to Mississippi, Margaret Garner jumped overboard with her infant. Crewmen pulled Garner out of the river. But the infant drowned. Margaret Garner died two years later of typhoid fever at 25 years of age.

HERO OF FREEDOM

LEVI COFFIN

(1789–1877)

LEVI COFFIN had witnessed the evils of slavery while growing up in the slave state of North Carolina. As a boy, he watched one day as slaves were marched along the road in chains. Young Coffin wondered what it would be like to have his own father taken away from him, like these slaves were taken from their families. Coffin vowed that day to fight against slavery. He got his first chance to do so as a teenager, while at a community corn-husking gathering. A slave trader had brought a slave to the corn husking, and Coffin helped the slave escape.

The antislavery views of Quakers such as the Coffins became increasingly unwelcome in North Carolina. Levi Coffin and his new wife, Catherine, decided to move to the free state of Indiana in 1826. There Levi Coffin opened a country store and became a successful merchant. The Coffin home in Newport, Indiana, was soon a busy Underground Railroad station. The couple helped thousands of fugitive slaves flee northward, and Levi Coffin earned the nickname "President of the Underground Railroad."

In 1847 the Coffins moved to Cincinnati, Ohio, to open a "free produce" warehouse. The cotton, sugar, and other goods sold from the warehouse were grown and harvested without slave labor. The Coffins also continued their Underground Railroad activities in Cincinnati. After the Civil War, the Coffins worked to educate former slaves.

Paying the Price

Like the Garners, many recaptured fugitive slaves were sold. Selling off "troublesome" slaves allowed the master to pass on his "untrustworthy property" to someone else. (Slave owners rarely told buyers that the slave had tried to run away.) It was also a clear warning to other slaves: Anyone who was caught trying to flee would be sold away. A returned runaway could expect other punishments as well. Brutal beatings and whippings were standard. Before

Andrew Jackson became president in 1829, one of his slaves escaped from his Tennessee plantation. In an ad placed in a newspaper, Jackson offered a $50 reward for the man's return "and ten dollars extra, for every hundred lashes any person will give him, to the amount of 300."

✥✥ *The last time I ran away [my master] caught me with his hounds, and I was torn badly by them. The day after my capture he came and looked hard at me, and setting his teeth together, hissed out, 'I'm going to cure you of this fever for running away, if I have to kill you to do it.' Then he got two big fellows to tie my hands together over the whipping post. He had my feet tied also, and in that position I was suspended by my hands so my feet barely touched the ground. All the whippings I have had were tame in comparison with this one. The lash was laid on until my back was perfectly raw, and it was only when I fainted that my cruel master stopped. When I became conscious, he glared at me, and grasping a large cat that was by, he dragged it across my back while its claws stuck into the flesh like so many fish-hooks . . . Well, then, he took and washed my back in spirits of turpentine . . . But all this ill-treatment only aroused me the more and as soon as my strength came back I started off again.*

▨ Henry Banks, *a former Virginia slave who, after many attempts, escaped to Canada*

THIS MURAL PORTRAYS THE DOOMED FLIGHT OF THE GARNERS ACROSS THE FROZEN OHIO RIVER.

There were many other punishments given to "cure" a slave of running away. Recaptured slaves were often locked up at night for months, hobbled by chained feet, or forced to wear iron collars with bells. Sometimes owners even used hot irons to brand their initials into the skin of captured slaves. That way, they could be more easily identified and returned if they fled again. Runaways who were caught far from their owner's homes were put in jail. The jailors tried to track down a fugitive's owner by posting or publishing an advertisement describing the

THE GRAVESTONE OF LEVI AND CATHERINE COFFIN
READS: *NOBLE BENFACTORS, AIDING THOUSANDS TO
GAIN FREEDOM. A TRIBUTE FROM THE COLORED PEOPLE
OF CINCINNATI.*

jailed runaway. When the owner came and claimed the slave, he was returned to his master. If no one claimed the slave, the slave was sold and the money was kept for the owner, in case he came to claim his property later.

With oaths and all sorts of vile language they commanded us to come out [of our hiding place] and deliver ourselves up, or else have our brains blown out. I said, "I will come out; but will not give myself up." I walked out, followed by Banks, feeling that my last moments had come . . . Mullen [the overseer] presented his gun at my breast and told me to surrender. I said, "Never; I'll die first," and striking the gun to one side . . . We both dashed through the creek, and as I climbed up the marsh on the other side, I received a full charge of [shotgun] shot in my right arm and leg, many of which have never been extracted. Banks was shot in the back and we both fell helpless to the ground, bathed in blood . . . [W]e were driven to King George county jail . . . We were put in the dungeon or cell where men condemned to be hung were kept, not a very cheerful place to be sure, but I could not help wishing I should meet that fate rather than be a slave again.

ISAAC D. WILLIAMS, a former slave who eventually escaped

Underground Railroad workers—and anyone else helping fugitives—put themselves at great risk. The fine for assisting or interfering with the arrest of a runaway slave was boosted from $500 to $1,000 with passage of the Fugitive Slave Law in 1850. Southern states also punished those aiding fugitives with hard-labor jail time. Underground Railroad conductor and minister Calvin Fairbanks spent 16 years in a Kentucky prison for helping a family of slaves escape to Canada. Another conductor, Charles Torrey, died of tuberculosis in a Baltimore, Maryland, prison after being arrested for aiding runaways. Torrey had conducted some 400 slaves to freedom. The shoemaker Samuel A. Smith, who nailed shut the crate in which Henry "Box" Brown (see page 67–68) was shipped to safety, was also caught. Smith spent seven years in prison for shipping two other runaways.

Jonathan Walker was a Massachusetts sea captain—and an abolitionist. In 1844 he tried to smuggle seven runaway slaves from Florida to the Bahamas, where slavery was outlawed. But Walker's boat was captured, and the slaves were returned to their owners. Captain Walker was jailed for eight months and was forced to pay the slave owners for damages. As further punishment, the letters "S.S." (for "slave stealer") were burned into the palm of Walker's right hand.

Delaware stationmaster Thomas Garrett (see page 89) was fined so heavily for aiding two

MAKE A PAPER QUILT BLOCK

HOMEMADE BLANKETS made from pieced-together scraps of fabric are called quilts. Quilt makers often stitch together small triangles and squares of fabric into a repeated pattern called a "quilt block." The completed blocks are then sewn together to make the decorative top of a quilt.

Some quilt makers used their sewing skills to help runaway slaves during Underground Railroad times. Like lanterns, painted chimneys, and other items, quilts were used as safe-house signals. A quilt hung in the front yard often meant that it was safe to approach an Underground Railroad station. But a quilt hung out back meant that danger was near. The block patterns themselves of some quilts passed on a message or reminder to fleeing slaves. Some showed flying geese, which slaves could follow northward in the spring, or sailing ships that crossed Lake Erie to Canada. Other quilts featured symbols of the Underground Railroad, such as the North Star or crossroads.

YOU'LL NEED
- Ruler
- Pencil or pen
- White paper
- Colored paper in several colors
- Scissors
- Glue

1. Using a ruler, draw an 8-inch (20-cm) square on the white paper. Divide the square into 16 2-inch (5-cm) squares—4 squares across the top and 4 along the side, creating a grid.

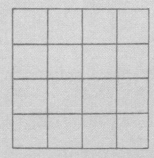

2. Cut out many squares of 2-inch-by-2-inch colored paper. Cut half of the squares in half diagonally, so that they become triangles.

3. Use the colored squares and triangles to create a quilt block pattern on the white grid. Try to create symbols or scenes that might help runaway slaves escape to freedom. Below are some examples. Think about the message your design might pass on to fugitive slaves.

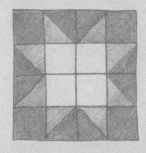

NORTH STAR

FLYING GEESE

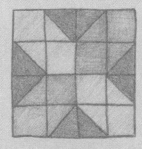

CROSSROADS

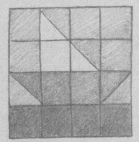

SAILING SHIP

4. Once you've created a pattern, you can make it permanent by gluing it onto another sheet of paper.

JANE JOHNSON.

fugitive slave children that, at age 60, he had to sell his business. But when someone scolded him about helping runaways, Garrett said, "Friend, I haven't a dollar in the world, but if thee knows a fugitive who needs a breakfast, send him to me." Garrett's Philadelphia partner, William Still (see page 79), was no stranger to the courtroom, either. After helping Jane Johnson and her two sons run away from their master, Still and others were charged with kidnapping and assault. Jane Johnson bravely returned to Philadelphia for the trial. Female abolitionists quickly escorted the fugitive mother into the courtroom under a veil to hide her identity. Once inside, Johnson announced to the courtroom that she hadn't been kidnapped. "I went away of my own free will," Johnson told the judge. "I always wished to be free and meant to be free when I came North . . . I had rather die than go back." Still was found not guilty. Jane Johnson eventually settled in Boston, Massachusetts, where her two sons attended school.

The punishments received by white abolitionists and Underground Railroad workers like Walker and Garrett might seem harsh. But they were mild compared to what happened to free blacks or former slaves who were convicted of aiding runaways. Often their worst nightmares came true—they were abducted and sold back into slavery. Even an escaped slave who'd been living in a free state for dozens of years wasn't safe. If claimed by a slave owner, the former slave would be sent back into slavery. That's what happened to John Mason. Mason was a former slave who'd escaped from Kentucky to Canada. But Mason left Canada and made many trips into slave states to conduct more than 1,000 slaves to freedom. The brave Underground Railroad conductor's luck ran out one fall day. He was helping four runaways toward the river when they heard the baying of hounds on their heels. Mason fought off the dogs until

WILLIAM STILL AND OTHER PHILADELPHIA UNDERGROUND RAILROAD WORKERS HELP JANE JOHNSON AND HER TWO SONS ESCAPE THEIR OWNER IN BROAD DAYLIGHT.

LIGHT A LANTERN

UNDERGROUND RAILROAD stationmasters used a number of signals to let fugitive slaves know that it was safe to approach their stations. Some, like the Rankins, of Ripley, Ohio, left a lamp lit in a window at night. Other stationmasters hung lit lanterns on gates and statues, where runaways could see them. In this activity you can make a simple candle lantern to light.

✂ *Adult supervision required*

YOU'LL NEED

☒ Utility scissors or knife
☒ Aluminum soda can
☒ Aluminum-foil (not plastic) duct tape
☒ Newspaper
☒ Pushpin
☒ Paper-hole punch
☒ 2 feet (61 cm) of thin wire
☒ Small votive or tea candle
☒ Needle-nose pliers
☒ Long fireplace matches

1. Ask an adult to use the utility scissors or a knife to carefully cut the top off the can. Cover the sharp edges with pieces of aluminum duct tape. (If you want to, you can cover the entire can with the tape.)

2. Stuff the can tightly with newspaper. This helps prevent the can from being crushed.

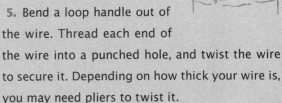

3. Using the pushpin, poke lots of holes in the sides of the can. These holes will let light through. If you like, you can make holes in decorative patterns.

4. Using the hole punch, punch a hole on either side of the can, about ½ inch (1 cm) from the top of the can. Make sure the holes are exactly opposite each other.

5. Bend a loop handle out of the wire. Thread each end of the wire into a punched hole, and twist the wire to secure it. Depending on how thick your wire is, you may need pliers to twist it.

6. Set the candle inside the lantern. Ask an adult to light the candle.

❗ BE SAFE: Never leave a lighted candle unattended.

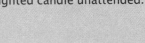
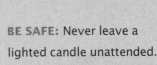

both his arms were broken and his body was ripped by teeth and claws. His captors sold him to a New Orleans trader and back into slavery. Miraculously, he somehow managed to escape again and return to freedom in Canada.

HERO OF FREEDOM

SAMUEL D. BURRIS

(1808–C. 1869)

SAMUEL D. BURRIS was born a free black in the slave state of Delaware. Burris moved his family to Philadelphia, Pennsylvania, where they became part of the city's large free black community. Burris began working as an Underground Railroad conductor in 1845. He traveled to the nearby slave states of Delaware and Maryland and guided escaped slaves into the free state of Pennsylvania. Burris worked closely with William Still, of the Pennsylvania Anti-Slavery Society. Many of the hundreds of runaways that Burris helped escape were sent along the Underground Railroad through Still's office.

Burris was caught aiding a fugitive in Delaware in the summer of 1847. He was jailed for about a year before he was finally tried. This left his family without a father and breadwinner. At the trial Burris was convicted of helping fugitives and sentenced to be auctioned off as a slave. Fortunately, his friends in the Underground Railroad were able to purchase him at that auction and set him free. After his brush with near slavery, Samuel Burris never ventured into a slave state again. In 1852 he moved his family to the free state of California. After the Civil War, Burris worked with African American churches to raise money to aid newly freed slaves.

Free blacks who helped fugitives were in no less danger than slaves in many Southern states. In the slave state of Delaware, the punishment for free blacks aiding runaways was being sold into slavery for seven years—if not forever. Samuel Burris was a free black Underground Railroad conductor who once said that "helping slaves to regain freedom . . . in the state of Delaware is a crime next to that of murder, if committed by a colored man." Burris was from Delaware, but he moved his family to Philadelphia, where he started conducting for the Underground Railroad. Burris helped hundreds of runaways to freedom. Unfortunately he was caught with fleeing slaves in Delaware, jailed, and sentenced to be sold as a slave.

Samuel Burris's friends and coworkers on the Underground Railroad came up with a plan to rescue him. Burris was put up for sale at a slave auction. What Burris didn't know was that one of the men inspecting his teeth and testing the strength of his legs was only pretending to be a slave trader. He was really an abolitionist who was there to buy Burris's freedom! The abolitionist outbid the real slave traders by $100 and got the bill of sale for purchasing Samuel Burris. Burris thought he was doomed until the abolitionist whispered in his ear that "all was right . . . he'd been bought with abolition gold to save him from going south."

The risk of being recaptured—or worse—was very real for runaways. It was perfectly legal in some Southern states for any citizen to shoot a runaway. And a great many fugitive slaves were jailed and returned to slavery. But often the punishment that recaptured runaways received only made them more determined to flee again. Many slaves who escaped to freedom didn't make it on the first try. They were caught, usually beaten and whipped, and often sold away from their families. Yet they attempted escape again and again. Staying in slavery seemed a far worse punishment than anything their masters could hand out. These "troublemaker" slaves didn't have "running away illness," as their owners claimed. They'd caught a far more serious "disease"—the desire for freedom.

The driver now came around and opened the door, saying, "boys, you are safe in Canada." I jumped out, followed by Banks and Nicholas, and we shouted and hallooed just like crazy folks, "We're free; we're free; bless the Lord for it; bless the Lord for it; blessings on his holy name." I then threw up my hat in the air and we all threw our arms around each other and cried for very joy, that seemed to well right up within us and find vent in this manner. We danced around like children and our actions excited the attention of people around us, who, when they found the cause of our extravagant actions, did not blame or make fun of them but cheered loudly, and I joined in, clapping my hands over our new-found happiness. Oh this grand, glorious liberty. You have only to be a slave once to appreciate freedom. It was a curious coincidence that the day we entered Canada as free men was Christmas, and what a glorious Christmas present we had; the highest boon a slave could have asked for—his liberty.

ISAAC D. WILLIAMS, a former slave who escaped with former slaves Henry Banks and Christopher Nicholas

RECAPTURED RUNAWAY SLAVES AND SLAVES BEING SOLD WERE OFTEN KEPT IN SLAVE JAILS OR SLAVE PENS LIKE THIS ONE IN ALEXANDRIA, VIRGINIA.

Brakemen

Making a Life in Freedom

AFTER THE FUGITIVE Slave Act became law in 1850, Harriet Tubman began conducting her passengers all the way to Canada. She usually led them through northern New York State, stopping at Underground Railroad stations in Albany, Syracuse, and Rochester. "Moses," as Tubman was called, and her "cargo" then crossed the border near Niagara Falls. A suspension bridge there spanned the Niagara River, which separates the two countries. Harriet never tired of gazing at the gigantic waterfall as she arrived again at freedom's gate.

Once in Canada, Harriet delivered the fugitives to St. Catharines. The Canadian town had a black community of about 800 people, most of whom had once been slaves themselves. Harriet had settled her brothers and sisters and their families in St. Catharines after rescuing them. During the 1850s, Harriet also made her home in St. Catharines when she wasn't conducting slaves out of the South. "We would rather stay in our native land, if we could be as free there as we are here," said Harriet. But it was just too dangerous in the United States—especially for those fugitives such as Harriet, whose capture, "dead or alive," would bring kidnappers huge rewards!

When in St. Catharines, Harriet did odd jobs to earn money. She also worked as an Underground Railroad "brakeman," helping newly free runaways find homes and work.

By 1857 Harriet had rescued much of her family. But her elderly parents were still in Maryland. Thankfully, they were no longer slaves. Her father, Ben Ross, was a free black, and he'd purchased his wife, Rit. (Rit's master sold her for only $20 because she was too old to work.) But Ben Ross was in a different kind of trouble. He had been arrested for helping a slave escape. Harriet couldn't let her father go to jail for doing Underground Railroad work. She had to get her parents to Canada—and soon. Because Ben and Rit Ross were too feeble to walk all night through swamps and woods, Harriet needed a wagon—and a horse and wagon cost money. Harriet went to the New York Anti-Slavery Office in search of friends with funds. "I'm not going to eat or drink till I get enough money to take me down after the old people," Harriet declared. By that afternoon, her friends raised $60, and Harriet was quickly on her way.

Once back in Maryland, Harriet bought an old horse and cobbled together a "freedom chariot" from an old buggy and some boards. Driving around the South with a buggy full of fugitives was risky. But they had no choice. Ben Ross was due in court the very next day! The three rode all night through Maryland. Once in Wilmington, Delaware, Harriet got some help from William Still and Thomas Garrett. Ben and Rit Ross made it safely to St. Catharines. Their children greeted them to freedom.

Harriet made her final rescue mission in late 1860. The winds of change were blowing in America. The United States had just elected a tall man named Abraham Lincoln as its new president. Many said the South would never stand for an antislavery president—they'd start a fight over it—and Harriet figured it might be her final chance to rescue her last sister left in slavery. Sadly, Harriet arrived in Maryland that December to the news that her sister had died. Seven other slaves answered her call to freedom, however, and Harriet conducted them to Canada. Safely back in St. Catharines, Harriet keep one eye looking South. They can talk about peace all they want, she told a friend. "I know there's going to be war."

The Last Stop

A runaway slave's final stop on the Underground Railroad was either a free state or a foreign country—usually Canada. Fleeing fugitives often reached this last stop exhausted and penniless. The men and women who helped newly arrived former slaves settle into a life of freedom were called brakemen. Like brakemen working on real trains, Underground Railroad brakemen helped their passengers' journeys come to a safe stop.

Many different kinds of people were Underground Railroad brakemen. Both men and women—black and white—were among those who helped former slaves find jobs and homes. Some brakemen were members of antislavery or church groups that were organized for the purpose of helping former slaves. Other brakemen were simply kind townspeople or farmers who were willing to help a fugitive slave find work and lodging.

Many runaways who escaped to free states in the North settled in cities and towns that had free black communities. These communities helped newly arrived fugitives find work and places to stay. The fugitives were often safer in free black communities because they blended in and avoided the attention of slave catchers passing through town. Large free black communities in cities such as Philadelphia and New

MOST FUGITIVE SLAVES ARRIVED AT THEIR FINAL UNDERGROUND RAILROAD STOP EXHAUSTED AND PENNILESS.

York had active vigilance committees that were constantly on the lookout for bounty hunters and fugitive-seeking lawmen.

A former slave who escaped to the free states no doubt lived better than he or she had while in slavery. But life in America for a free black in the early 1800s wasn't easy. No African American—free or slave—anywhere in the United States could vote. The U.S. Supreme Court's Dred Scott decision (see page 15) made

PHŒNIX FOUNDRY.

PARKER & HOOD,
Manufacturers of

Steam Engines

MILL GEARING, SUGAR MILLS & PANS,
THRESHING MACHINE AND ALL KINDS OF

IRON & BRASS CASTINGS,
REPAIRING DONE TO ORDER,
FRONT STREET, RIPLEY, O.

JOHN PARKER WAS A SUCCESSFUL BUSINESSMAN AND INVENTOR WHO LIVED IN OHIO, A FREE STATE. BUT AS A BLACK MAN, HE COULD NOT VOTE UNTIL 1870.

tice were commonplace. Northern whites might have been against slavery. But few whites saw blacks as equals.

Charlotte Forten was from a wealthy free black family. She wrote in her diary of being refused service at two Philadelphia ice cream shops in 1857. "Oh, how terribly I felt! . . . It is dreadful! dreadful! I cannot stay in such a place," wrote 19-year old Forten. William Still was well respected by many in Philadelphia. But as a black person, he was legally denied a ride on a streetcar many times.

Free blacks dealt with discrimination by setting up separate communities. African Americans started their own schools and newspapers. Free blacks ran businesses and stores that served and employed blacks. These black communities understood the connection between Northern racism and Southern slavery. Slavery would never end until people saw African Americans as equals. Racism, like slavery, was wrong. Many former slaves and free blacks in the North worked for the right of blacks to vote, the desegregation of streetcars, and tax money to fund black schools.

it clear: Blacks were not American citizens. Blacks weren't allowed in schools, and they were often not allowed to testify in court. Free blacks were often turned away from jobs as well as from churches, streetcars, stores, and other businesses. Discrimination, racism, and injus-

Oh, Canada!

Many free blacks were not satisfied with living as noncitizens in the United

States. They decided to move to a place where they could vote and own land—Canada. Philip Younger was a former slave who lived in Chatham, Canada. He explained, "Before I came here, I resided in the free States . . . [B]ut I feel better here—more like a man—I know I am—than in the States."

✧ *I came away from Virginia because I didn't like the condition of things there. I didn't like to be trod upon. A colored man there, let him be free born or not, must have a scrap of paper in his pocket to show that he is free . . . I don't see anything in the way of our doing a good business here [in Canada]. We employ twelve or fourteen hands now, and have white & black boys at work . . . There are four of us in the firm, all colored men . . . I think the colored people, after a while, will surmount the prejudice against them.*

▨ JOHN H. HILL, free black who moved to Canada

Canada began phasing out slavery in 1793 thanks to John Graves Simcoe. Simcoe was a British officer who fought in the Revolutionary War. While fighting against American Patriots, he saw how cruelly slaves were treated. Simcoe became an abolitionist. When Simcoe became the first Lieutenant Governor of Upper Canada (Ontario), he passed legislation that would phase out slavery. The Anti-Slavery Act of 1793

JOHN H. HILL SETTLED IN TORONTO, CANADA.

stated that slaves already in the province would remain enslaved until death. But no new slaves could be brought into Upper Canada, and children born to female slaves would be freed at age 25. The act was the first to limit slavery in the British Empire and helped bring about the Emancipation Act of 1833 that abolished slavery in all of Britain, including Canada and the other colonies.

Unlike the free states, Canada was a true haven for runaways. The American government had asked Canada to help retrieve escaped slaves. The United States wanted Canada to return fugitives and let slave catchers and lawmen enter Canada to look for their runaways.

FRANCIS ELLEN WATKINS HARPER WAS A FREE BLACK WOMAN WHO BECAME A FAMOUS POET. SHE MOVED FROM MARYLAND TO PENNSYLVANIA WHEN THE 1850 FUGITIVE SLAVE LAW MADE LIFE MORE DANGEROUS FOR FREE BLACKS IN THE SOUTH.

WAS COMMITTED

to the jail of Covington County, on the 26th day of June, 1836, by G. D. Gere, Esq., A negro man who says his name is Josiah, that he belongs to Mr. John Martin, living in Louisiana, twenty miles below Nathchez. Josiah is five feet eight inches high, heavy built, copper colour; his back very much scarred with the whip, and branded on the thigh and hips in three or four places thus: 'j.M.' or 'J.M.' The 'M' is very plain, but the 'j' or 'J' is not plain. The rim of his right ear has been bitten or cut off. He is about 31 years of age. Had on, when committed, pantaloons, made of bed-ticking, cotton coat, and an old fur hat very much worn. The owner of the above described negro is requested to comply requisitions of law, in such, cases made and provided for.

—J. L. JOLLEY, Sheriff, C. C.

FROM THE CLINTON, MISSISSIPPI, *GAZETTE*, JULY 23, 1836.

Canada refused, and the country made it clear that any slave who reached Canadian soil was free. After the Fugitive Slave Act became law, more and more runaways—and free blacks—headed to Canada. The free states were no longer safe. Slave hunters and federal lawmen were combing the North for runaways, and kidnappers were capturing free blacks and selling them down South.

I left Charleston in September, 1853. I lived in the free States some months, but finally left on account of the Fugitive Slave Bill. This was a law of tyranny . . . I had to come to Canada . . . I would rather die than go back,—that's a settled point with me—not on account of ill-treatment of the person; but I could not stand the idea of being held by another man as a chattel. Slavery itself is cruel enough, without regard to the hardships which slaves in general have to undergo.

WILLIAM L. HUMBERT, a former slave who settled near Windsor, Canada

While Canada was much safer than the free states, fugitive slaves still had to be careful. It was illegal for slave catchers to cross into Canada. But profitable rewards tempted some to break the law. Being kidnapped from Canada was rare, but not unheard of. There were also instances of slave catchers tricking fugitives to cross the border, back into the United States, where they could be captured. Many fugitives living in Canada changed their names and told only trusted friends about their pasts.

John Anderson was born a slave in Missouri. He ran away after his master sold him away from his wife and child. Anderson fled north, vowing not to be taken back to slavery alive. He narrowly escaped an attack by a white man who suspected that Anderson was a runaway. The men fought, and Anderson stabbed his attacker with a knife. Anderson escaped to Canada, unaware that the man he had stabbed later died. There was now a large reward out for John Anderson's arrest.

Once in Windsor, Canada, John Anderson attended a school for former slaves. One of the teachers there was the Underground Railroad conductor Laura Haviland (see page 66). Anderson told Haviland how much he missed his wife and child. Could she help them get to Canada as well? Haviland wrote a letter to Anderson's father-in-law and mailed it from her Michigan home. A few months later, two men came to her house. They claimed to have safely smuggled Anderson's family out of slavery and brought them to Detroit. All Anderson had to do was cross over the border into Detroit to meet them.

Laura Haviland was not easily fooled. She suspected that the men were really slave hunters, and that Anderson's family wasn't really waiting for him in Detroit—and she was right. Haviland telegrammed John Anderson, telling him that he was in danger and advising him to move farther away from the border. Anderson moved to Chatham, Canada, and changed his name. But soon the slave hunters crossed the border and began asking for him in Chatham. Blacks living in Chatham quickly figured out that the men were slave hunters. Anderson was able to get out of town before they found him. Sadly, Anderson was arrested five years later after a neighbor turned him in. The United States and Canada fought over Anderson as he sat in jail for a year, awaiting trial for murder. The United States demanded that he be returned because he was a criminal. Canada claimed that Anderson had killed in self-defense. After a number of trials, Anderson was finally set free.

Life Up North

Once the Underground Railroad deposited fleeing slaves in Canada, the fugitives' struggle changed. Instead of fearing for their lives and running from bloodhounds and slave catchers, the newly arrived immigrants had to worry about surviving. Most came to Canada with no money or possessions. The fugitives had escaped slavery, but they now found themselves in an unfamiliar land full of strangers.

It was the 28th of October, 1830, in the morning, when my feet first touched the Canada shore. I threw myself on the ground, rolled in the sand, seized handfuls of it and kissed them, and danced around . . . I hugged and kissed my wife and children, and, until the first exuberant burst of feeling was over, went on as before. There was not much time to be lost, though, in frolic even, at this extraordinary moment. I was a stranger in a strange land, and had to look about me at once for refuge and resource . . . I knew nothing about the country or the people, but kept my eyes and ears open, and made such inquiries as opportunity afforded.

Rev. Josiah Henson, a former slave and an Underground Railroad conductor and brakeman

Josiah Henson began looking for work the morning after his family arrived in Canada. Like most former slaves, Henson had never been to school. But he was a hard worker, and a local farmer soon hired him. Henson and his family moved into one of the shacks on the farm—after moving out the pigs that'd been living there! His wife laughed that it was better than the dirt-floor cabin they'd lived in as slaves. The newly free family piled straw in corners for beds, and they slept well.

Fugitive slaves like the Hensons worked at all kinds of jobs in Canada. Many used the skills they'd learned as slaves to get jobs on farms or to find work as cooks, maids, barbers, masons, or seamstresses. Canada wanted to encourage immigrants to move there, so land was made cheap and plentiful. Many former slaves were able to save enough money to buy land after a few years and farm for themselves.

Like the Hensons, many former slaves had only themselves to depend upon. But as the communities of former slaves in Canada grew, refugee associations sprang up and helped a number of former slaves settle in, find work, and sometimes buy land. The number of runaways streaming into Canada increased even more after the Fugitive Slave Act became law in 1850.

I had [six] dollars when I crossed over to Canada, and when I got to Chatham, I had five shillings. I hired out to a contractor on a railroad for eight shillings a day, and worked for him until about October, and then went to work as a waiter in a hotel, and got $10 a month. After I left there, I went to work barbering, and in November, 1853, came to London [Canada]. I had then clothed myself well, and saved eight or nine dollars besides. I went to work here for eight dollars a week and my board. About Christmas, I went to work for another man, who gave me $26 a month; and then the man sold out to me and another man, we giving him $350 for his shop. Since then,

JOSIAH HENSON

(1789–1883)

JOSIAH HENSON was born a slave in Maryland. As a very young boy he'd watched as his father was brutally whipped and his ear was cut off. Henson's father received this punishment because he'd tried to defend Henson's mother, who'd been assaulted by the overseer. Henson was sold away from his mother at age six, and he was sold again and again during his life as a slave.

While he was a slave, Henson married and became a preacher in the Methodist Episcopal Church. He was a valuable slave who helped manage the plantation he lived on. Henson made a deal with his master to buy his freedom. But his master later backed out of the agreement and decided to sell Henson. Josiah Henson wasn't going to be separated from his family. He fled with his wife and four children. After a long journey, they crossed into Canada in 1830.

Henson was taught to read and write by his son, who went to school in Canada. Josiah Henson became a minister in Dresden, Canada, and a leader in the Canadian black community, helping many new arrivals settle in the new land. In 1842 Josiah Henson established the Dawn Institute, an industrial school for refugees. Henson also became a conductor on the Underground Railroad. He made a number of trips back into the South, leading groups of as many as 30 fugitives to Canada.

In 1949 the story of Henson's life was published in the book *The Life of Josiah Henson, Formerly a Slave, Now an Inhabitant of Canada.* The slave narrative was read by Harriet Beecher Stowe, the author of *Uncle Tom's Cabin.* She later referred to Henson in her book *Key to Uncle Tom's Cabin,* and he became known as "the real Uncle Tom"—the man who Stowe had based her character on. Henson's autobiography became one of the most popular slave narratives ever published, and he met celebrities in America and Britain, including Queen Victoria.

I have been doing very well. I have bought a house and lot, for which I paid $1800. I have never had any trouble since I came to Canada. I have got a very good shop, and am doing as well as I could expect. I would not change my situation under any consideration. I would rather die than exchange freedom in Canada for slavery.

⊠ Isaac Throgmorton, a former Kentucky slave who lived in Chatham, Canada

⟨⊠⟩ *As any one would judge, the mass of our population are labourers. Some are most excellent mechanics and artisans; others are farmers, yeomen . . . A few in large towns are servants in hotels. A small number of the same class are servants on steamers. Exceedingly few of either sex, as compared with the coloured people of the neighbouring States, are household servants. This last fact, in connection with another I am about to mention, speaks well both for their independence and for the degree of equality existing betwixt whites and blacks in Canadian towns. There are a great many, as compared with what one sees in the States, engaged in other than menial or semi-menial employments—fewer barbers, bootblacks, and more porters, carters, cabowners, [etc.]. Small shopkeepers, also, are far more numerous, in proportion to their relative numbers, in Canada than in the States. Some of the grocers' shops, as well as those of other tradesmen, are on*

HERO OF FREEDOM

SAMUEL RINGGOLD WARD

(1817–C. 1866)

SAMUEL RINGGOLD WARD was born a slave in Maryland. His parents fled slavery with Ward when he was a young child. The family eventually settled in New York City, where Ward went to the African Free School. Among his classmates were a number of boys who grew up to be important African American abolitionists and leaders, including Henry Highland Garnet (see page 51). As a teenager, Ward worked as a clerk for the abolitionist David Ruggles (see page 98). He was beaten by a mob because of his antislavery views. The violent experience only strengthened Samuel Ringgold Ward's desire to end slavery.

Ward became a famous speaker for the American and New York Anti-Slavery societies and a campaigner for the antislavery Liberty Party. He also became a Congregational minister and the editor of a newspaper in Syracuse, New York. While in Syracuse, Ward helped a captured fugitive slave escape from jail. Ward and a number of other African Americans who'd helped the fugitive escape, including Jermain Wesley Loguen (see page 101), had to flee to Canada to avoid being arrested for their crime.

Once in Canada, Ward worked to help former slaves find work and homes. He also put his public speaking skills to work for the Anti-Slavery Society of Canada, and he founded the newspaper the *Provincial Freeman*. Ward wrote in his autobiography, "What I affirm of the Canadian Negro is, that he bears himself equal to English, Irish, Scotch, Dutch, or French Canadians, although he has and they have not been slaves; all I claim for the Canadian Negro is, that same fair rule and standard of character which is applied to other peoples, and by which they are estimated. Let us stand or fall by such a rule, and I am content."

a very respectable scale, considering the wants of the populace; many are equal to any in the colony. If any class excel, it is our mechanics and artisans.

⊠ SAMUEL RINGGOLD WARD, an abolitionist and Underground Railroad brakeman

Equal Under the Law

Blacks in Canada had the same rights as white immigrants under the law. Former slaves living in Canada could vote, own land, and serve on juries. Blacks and whites had the same rights in court as well. Blacks could accuse whites of crimes and testify against them. The children of blacks in Canada could legally go to public school and college, too.

❖ *[T]the law makes no difference between black & white. If it had not been for that, I would not have gone to Canada. If a man spits upon us or insults us, we knock him down, and the law will treat us fairly. We can't do that in the States.*

⊠ THOMAS LIKERS, a former Maryland slave who lived in Toronto, Canada

THESE REFUGEES FROM U.S. SLAVERY SETTLED IN WINDSOR, CANADA. FROM LEFT TO RIGHT ARE ANNE MARY JANE HUNT, MANSFIELD SMITH, LUCINDA SEYMOUR, HENRY STEVENSON, AND BUSH JOHNSON.

But many former slaves living in Canada did face discrimination and prejudice from their new white neighbors. Canada was a sparsely populated land, and its laws weren't always easily enforced. The law said that blacks and whites were equal. But newly arrived blacks weren't always treated equally by the local people.

I went to a church one Sabbath, & and sexton asked me, "What do you want here to-day?" I said, "Is there not to be service here to-day?" He said, "Yes, but we don't want any niggers here." I said, "You are mistaken in the man. I am not a 'nigger', but a negro." Eight years ago, I was driven out of Wallaceburg, which is near Dresden, by a mob of lumbermen, simply because of my color, and there have been two or three colored men driven out of their houses, near Ridgetown. I built a new house three years ago, which was all paid for, and the day it was finished, some person put a match to it, and it was burned.

Lewis C. Chambers, a former Maryland slave who lived in Canada

Canada was a land of many new immigrants. Some Canadians welcomed the refugees from slavery and wanted to help them get settled. Others resented the newcomers because they believed that they'd take work away from them. Many Canadian immigrants from Europe had never seen black people before, and they were perhaps wary of them. Others held racist beliefs and didn't want their children "mixing" with blacks at school. But most Canadians probably had no strong feelings one way or the other about the fugitives from the South. Like everyone else, they were busy getting by in a new land.

I left Maryland with my wife and two children in 1851 . . . I look at slavery as the most horrid thing on earth. It is awful to think of the poor slaves panting for a place of refuge, and so few able to find it. There is not a day or night that I don't think about them, and wish that slavery might be abolished, and every man have his God-given rights . . . I have prospered well in freedom. I thank the Lord for my success here. I own fifty acres of land, bought and paid for by my own energy and exertions, and I have the deed in my house . . . I own two span of horses, twelve head of hogs, six sheep, two milk cows, and am putting up a farm barn . . . There is a great deal of prejudice here . . . Still, we have more freedom here than in the United States, as far as the government law guarantees.

William Henry Bradley, a former slave who settled in Dresden, Canada

Where the Fugitives Settled

Most of the fugitive slaves who escaped to Canada settled near the Canadian–United States border. The runaways had journeyed far enough just to cross the border. They didn't have money to travel farther into Canada. And some didn't want to go any farther than necessary to be free. Many hoped that someday their own country would end the evil of slavery, and they'd be able to return to the United States.

Fugitive slaves coming into Canada from Ohio crossed Lake Erie. Those coming overland through Michigan into Canada went around Lake Erie. These paths brought the runaways to the strip of land sandwiched between Lake Huron and Lake Erie. The former slaves settled into Canadian cities such as Windsor—which lay just across the river from Detroit, Michigan—as well as Chatham, Sandwich, Buxton, Dresden, and London. (See map at right.)

By the 1850s, former slaves made up a good percentage of these towns. Chatham was a town of about 4,000 people at the time. It was said to have about 800 black residents in town, and another 1,200 in the surrounding area. It was in Chatham that Mary Ann Shadd Cary (see left) ran the *Provincial Freeman*. Cary, a free black in the United States, had emigrated to Canada. Her newspaper urged fugitives and free black Americans to move to Canada, get educated, and be self-reliant.

Runaway slaves who escaped from the United States via New York State—such as Har-

---

HERO OF FREEDOM

MARY ANN SHADD CARY
(1823–1893)

MARY ANN SHADD CARY was born a free black in Delaware. Her parents were abolitionists. Her father sold subscriptions to William Lloyd Garrison's *The Liberator* (see page 41) and was an Underground Railroad stationmaster who hid runaways in the family home. As a slave state, Delaware forbid the education of African Americans. At age 10, Cary went to Pennsylvania to attend a Quaker school.

Cary became a teacher and a writer. She moved to Canada after the passage of the Fugitive Slave Act. There she and her sister-in-law opened a school in Windsor for all children—black and white, boys and girls. Cary didn't believe that people should be segregated or treated differently because of their race or sex. In 1853 she started the newspaper the *Provincial Freeman* in Chatham, Canada, making Cary the first black North American female editor and publisher. Cary wrote antislavery articles for the newspaper in which she urged American blacks to move to Canada. She also wrote in support of women's rights. (At the time, women of all races couldn't vote in either Canada or the United States.)

After the start of the Civil War, Cary returned to the United States to recruit blacks for the Union army. After the war ended and slavery was abolished, Cary and her family moved to Washington, D.C., where she became the first female African American lawyer. Cary spent the rest of her life fighting for the rights of women and African Americans.

WHERE FORMER SLAVES SETTLED IN 1800s CANADA

CANADA

Lake Huron

Toronto ■

Lake Ontario

■ London

St. Catharines

Niagara Falls

Fort Erie

NEW YORK

MICHIGAN

■ Dresden

■ Chatham

Windsor ■ ■ Buxton

Sandwich

Lake Erie

PENNSYLVANIA

OHIO

UNITED STATES

SAMUEL HARPER AND HIS WIFE WERE MISSOURI SLAVES WHO ESCAPED FROM THE UNITED STATES IN THE WINTER OF 1858–1859 AND SETTLED IN WINDSOR, CANADA.

riet Tubman's passengers—often settled along the Canadian side of Lake Ontario. The Canadian towns of St. Catharines, Niagara Falls, and Fort Erie were just across the border from Buffalo, New York. The Canadian city of Toronto is also near the United States border. The city became home to at least 1,000 refugees from slavery. The former slaves built a thriving community in Toronto, with three black churches and a debating club.

Refugee Settlements

The Reverend William King was a Presbyterian missionary working in Canada who believed that slavery was wrong. But in 1846 he suddenly became a slave owner. King inherited the slaves from his father-in-law, a Louisiana planter. King was the only living heir to his father-in-law's property, which included 15 enslaved human beings. He traveled to Louisiana to claim the slaves and free them. But King wanted the 15 new free blacks to have a better life—a chance to own land, vote, and send their children to school. So King offered to bring the former slaves back with him to Canada to live.

The new black settlers inspired King to start Elgin Settlement, a planned community for fugitive slaves. With the help of the Presbyterian Church and Canada's Governor General Lord Elgin, King was granted 9,000 acres (3,600 hectares) of forested land just 12 miles (19 kilometers) south of Chatham, Canada. The land was divided into 50-acre (20 hectare) lots that black settlers could buy for $2.50 an acre and pay for over a 10-year period. Settlers had to agree to build a house on the land and to follow certain rules, including having no liquor. Elgin Settlement quickly grew into a successful community. Families worked together to clear land and build log homes. Fields of wheat and gardens of vegetables were planted and soon harvested.

Within a year, Elgin Settlement had a post office and a church. Before long, the community boasted a store, a two-story hotel, a blacksmith, a carpenter, shoe shops, factories, and a bank. Most important, Elgin Settlement had both an elementary school and a secondary school. The schools at Elgin Settlement became

HERO OF FREEDOM

REV. WILLIAM KING

(1812–1895)

WILLIAM KING was born, raised, and went to college in Ireland. When his family immigrated to America, William King moved with them. King found a teaching job at an academy for children of wealthy families in the South. He eventually married a Southern woman whose father was a slave owner. King believed that slavery was wrong, and he was horrified at the harsh treatment of slaves in the South. He didn't want to raise his children in a country that allowed slavery, so he moved his young family to Scotland, where he studied to be a minister. Tragically, his wife, son, and infant daughter all died within a short time of each other soon after.

King finished his studies, became a Presbyterian minister, and was sent to Canada as a missionary. After finding out that he'd inherited 15 slaves from the father of his late wife, King brought them to Canada. They became the first residents of King's Elgin Settlement. The village was later renamed Buxton, in honor of the famous English abolitionist Sir Thomas Fowell Buxton, who helped outlaw slavery in Britain and all its colonies. In 1880 King moved to Chatham, where he lived until his death.

the best, and white parents soon wanted their children to attend them as well. Teachers came from the Presbyterian college in Toronto to teach the students Latin and Greek. Black graduates from Elgin Settlement's secondary school grew up to become doctors, teachers, missionaries, lawyers, and even a state representative of Alabama.

⚇ *My two oldest children go to school. The oldest is well along, and studies Latin and Greek. The other three are not old enough to go to school. We have good schools here,—music and needlework are taught . . . I think my present condition here far preferable to what it would have been in slavery. There we were in darkness,—here we are in light. My children also would have grown up, had I remained there, in ignorance and darkness.*

▨ MRS. ISAAC RILEY, a former Missouri slave who escaped and settled with her family in Elgin Settlement

With a population of 2,000 people by the 1860s, Elgin Settlement was probably the most successful planned refugee community in Canada. But it wasn't the only one. Wilberforce Settlement was a planned community started by former slaves. Henry Bibb (see page 126) was himself a fugitive slave who founded the Refugees' Home Society near Windsor. The planned community sold 25-acre lots to black settlers. It also had a school, where the Underground Railroad conductor Laura Smith Haviland taught.

Schools were a big reason that many refugees moved to the planned settlements. Former slaves who'd been forbidden to learn to read and write wanted their children to be educated. Children of all races were supposed to be allowed in Canada's public schools. But black children weren't always admitted or welcome— and few fugitive slaves could afford to pay for private schooling. The Dawn Institute was built near Dresden to provide blacks an education. Established by former slave Josiah Henson (see page 118) and abolitionist Hiram Wilson (see page 129), the school taught both academic subjects and job skills including the milling of lumber and flour. Once fugitive slaves heard about the school they moved nearby. By the 1850s the area surrounding the Dawn Institute had become a community, known as Dawn, of 500 people.

⚇ *I removed to Dawn, and was elected one of the trustees of the school in that place. From Dawn I came to Chatham about 1849. Chatham was then a little village of frame buildings and log cabins . . . [Now t]here are four churches of colored people which are well filled. We have separate schools which are tolerably well attended,—*

860

FUGITIVE SLAVES
IN CANADA.

THE ELGIN SETTLEMENT.

THERE WILL BE A PUBLIC MEETING IN

FREE SOUTH LEITH CHURCH,
ON
THURSDAY EVENING NEXT, AT 7 O'CLOCK,
TO HEAR STATEMENTS FROM

THE REV. WILLIAM KING,
formerly a Slave Owner in Louisiana, United States, and
WILLIAM H. DAY, ESQ. M.A.,
A Deputation from Canada, whither the Thirty Thousand have fled, escaping from American Slavery.

The Rev. WILLIAM KING liberated his own Slaves, and in this respect is mentioned in Mrs Harriet Beecher Stowe's work, "Dred," as "Clayton."

As this is a work of general benevolence—simply to give the Bible to those in Canada who have heretofore been deprived of it—it is hoped that there will be a large attendance at the Meeting.

Leith, 26th November 1859.   Burrell & Dyers, Printers, Leith.

HENRY BIBB

(1815–1854)

HENRY BIBB was born a slave in Kentucky. Bibb's escape attempts were many—he claimed to have escaped from seven different owners! His first success came in his early 20s when he fled to Cincinnati, Ohio. But when he returned six months later to help his wife and child escape, he was caught. After being sold, running away, and recaptured a number of times, Bibb finally successfully escaped to Detroit, Michigan. There he went to school and eventually became a popular speaker. He was soon lecturing to abolitionist organizations and campaigning for the antislavery Liberty party. In 1849 he published his autobiography, *Narrative of the Life and Adventures of Henry Bibb, an American Slave*. He also wrote a number of letters to his former owner. One said, "You may perhaps think hard of us for running away from slavery, but as to myself, I have but one apology to make for it, which is this: I have only to regret that I did not start at an earlier period."

After the passage of the Fugitive Slave Law in 1850, Bibb no longer felt safe in Detroit. He moved across the border to Windsor, Canada, and urged other slaves and free blacks to come to Canada, too. In 1851 Bibb began publishing one of Canada's first black newspapers, the *Voice of the Fugitive*. Bibb helped organize the Refugees' Home Society, a group that purchased thousands of acres of land to start a settlement for former slaves.

the Sunday school is very numerously attended. There are three charitable societies of men, and two of women, which do much good, relieving the wants of the sick and destitute. There is a great deal of property owned here by the colored people: their number has doubled in two years, mainly by immigration, which continues still—

especially of fugitive slaves,—sometimes twenty in one day . . . Our children growing up in this country, and not having the fear of any white man, and being taught to read and write, will grow up entirely different from their fathers,—of more benefit to themselves, of more benefit to the government, and will be more able to set good examples to the rising generation. Intelligent parents will raise up intelligent children.

▨ J. C. Brown, a former slave who settled in Chatham, Canada

Proving the Proslavers Wrong

Most slaves who escaped to Canada settled in towns, cities, and settlements in and around the Great Lakes. The area was called Canada West back then. Today it's the province of Ontario. But some crossed the Canadian border via New England states that lay farther east. They settled in towns in areas that would become Quebec and Nova Scotia. No one knows for sure how many fugitive slaves moved to Canada. Few who worked in the Underground Railroad wanted to keep records that might get them arrested. The total number of runaways living in Canada by the 1860s was probably somewhere between 20,000 and 40,000 people.

CANADA TODAY

MOST OF THE FUGITIVE slaves who escaped to Canada settled in what was then called Canada West. Today the section of Canada that borders the Great Lakes is called Ontario. Ontario is one of the 10 provinces and three territories that make up modern Canada. Find out more about our neighbor to the north by first naming the provinces and territories of Canada. Then use the chart to find out where Canadians of African descent live today.

YOU'LL NEED
- Photocopier or tracing paper
- Pen with black ink
- Red, orange, and yellow colored pens or pencils
- Encyclopedia or book about Canada

1. Make a copy of the map of Canada found on page 128. You can make a photocopy of it, or you can trace it using tracing paper.

2. Find out the names and locations of the 10 Canadian provinces and three territories. Using the pen, label them on the map.

3. Now use the chart here to color the provinces and territories based on their black populations.

- *Color the province that has a black population of higher than 3 percent red.*

- *Color the provinces that have a black population of between 2 and 3 percent orange.*

- *Color the provinces that have a black population of between 1 and 2 percent yellow.*

- *Leave uncolored those provinces and territories that have a black population of less than 1 percent.*

Where do most Canadians of African descent live today?

Continued on next page . . .

CANADIAN PROVINCE OR TERRITORY	BLACK POPULATION IN 2001	continued from previous column	
Alberta	1.1%	Nova Scotia	2.2%
British Columbia	.7%	Nunavut	.2%
Manitoba	1.2%	Ontario	3.6%
New Brunswick	.5%	Prince Edward Island	.3%
Newfoundland (and Labrador)	.2%	Quebec	2.1%
Northwest Territories	.5%	Saskatchewan	.4%
		Yukon	.4%

continued in next column

. . . continued from previous page

Greenland

Alaska

CANADA

UNITED STATES

On the twenty-sixth [of September 1844] we passed over to Windsor, on the Canada side . . . [W]e visited a number of colored families, many of whom recognized me at once, having been at my house in the days of their distress when fleeing from a land of whips and chains . . . We visited all the principal settlements of fugitives in Canada West . . . We spent nearly two months in this way, traveling from place to place on horseback, as there were no railroads in that section then . . . Some of them were well situated, owned good farms, and were perhaps worth more than their former masters . . . but there was much destitution and suffering among those who had recently come in. Many fugitives arrived weary and footsore, with their clothing in rags, having been torn by briers and bitten by dogs on their way, and when the precious boon of freedom was obtained, they found themselves possessed of little else, in a country unknown to them and a climate much colder than that to which they were accustomed . . . At the time of our visit, in 1844, there was said to be about 40,000 fugitives in Canada who had escaped from Southern bondage.

LEVI COFFIN, an Underground Railroad stationmaster

Regardless of their exact number, every slave who had struggled to escape to Canada and was living well as a free person sent a powerful message to the United States. The communities of former slaves in Canada proved the South's claims wrong. They proved that slaves were not content in slavery, as many Southerners claimed, and that African Americans were perfectly fine without the "care" that slave owners claimed they needed.

The African American Underground Railroad agent, stationmaster, and brakeman William Still (see page 79) visited Canada in 1855. He wanted to see for himself where he was sending fugitive slaves on the Underground Railroad. William Still saw many former slaves living good lives in Canada. He relayed his positive report to abolitionist societies and used the examples of successful blacks in Canada to argue for the freeing of all slaves. If slaves were freed, Still argued, they'd become hardworking citizens who would help America grow. The refugee communities in Canada proved it.

Thousands of former slaves made a home for themselves in Canada. Some would live the rest of their lives there, vowing never to return to the country that had enslaved them from birth. But many hoped to return to the United States someday. Most still had family and friends across the border. But they wouldn't go back until they could be free in America. Was that day coming? There were rumors that war was on the way—a civil war between the Northern and Southern states. Would such a

war end slavery? Or would it just give the slaveholders their own separate country? Canada's newest black citizens watched and listened nervously as war loomed in their former homeland.

HERO OF FREEDOM

HIRAM WILSON

(1803–1864)

HIRAM WILSON was born in New Hampshire in 1803. While studying to become a minister, he joined an abolitionist group and finished his studies at Oberlin College in Ohio, a famous hotbed of antislavery sentiment. Wilson moved to Toronto, Canada, in the 1830s to work for the American Anti-Slavery Society. In 1842 he joined Josiah Henson to establish the Dawn Institute, a school near Dresden, Canada.

Wilson eventually settled in St. Catharines, Canada, where he became an abolitionist leader and an Underground Railroad brakeman. There Wilson ran an evening school and relief station for newly arrived fugitive slaves called the Refugee Slaves' Friends Society. Many of the runaway slaves that Harriet Tubman led to St. Catharines were aided by Wilson. He explained in a letter, "The object of the society is to bear testimony against slavery by extending sympathy and friendly aid to refugees from slavery who from time to time are taking shelter in this section of Canada and by promoting the education of their children . . . The enslavement of man is a flagrant sin against God and an outrage upon humanity, not to be countenanced by civilized people who reverance the name of God or bear the Christian name."

6

CHAPTER

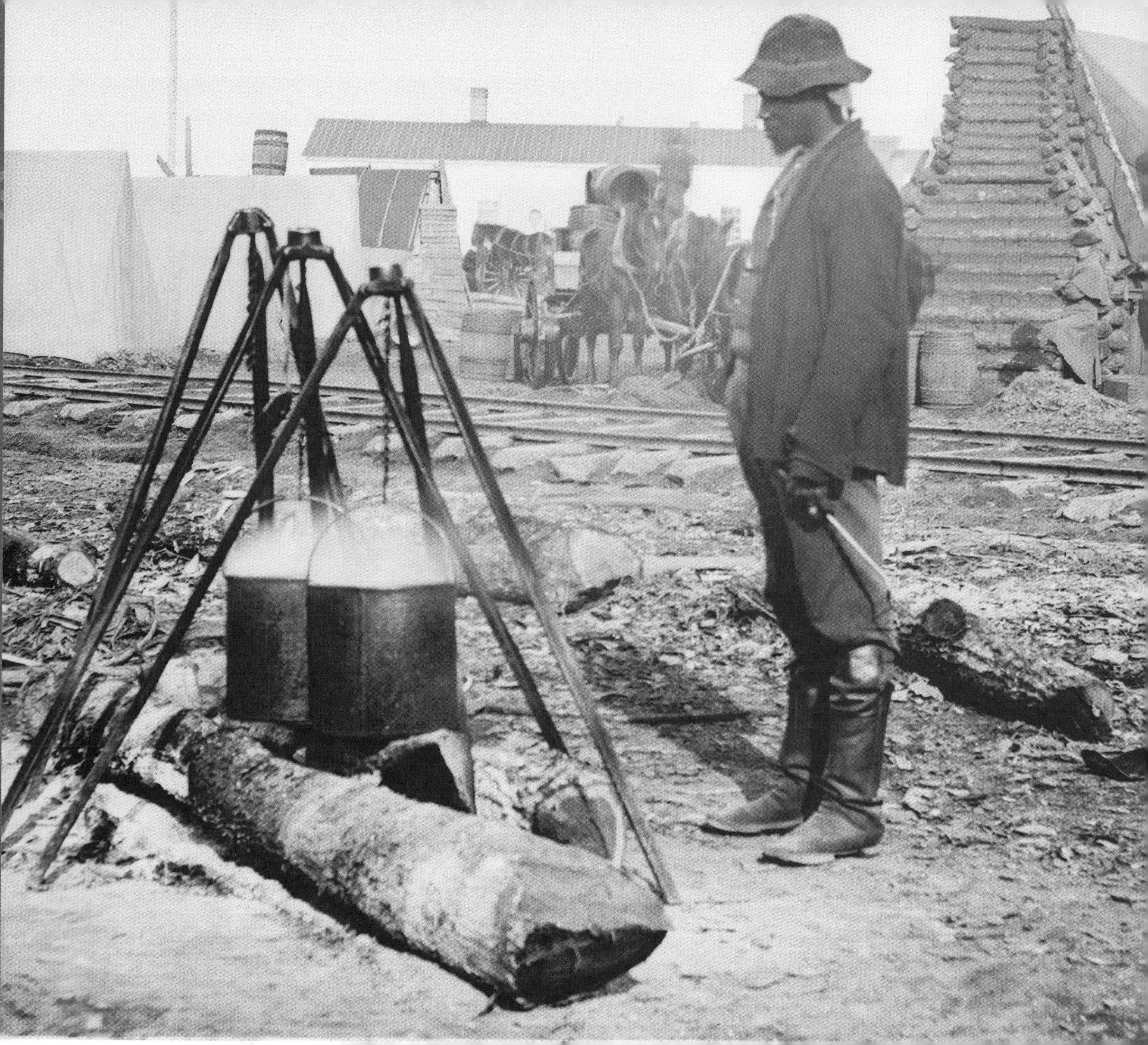

End of the Line

War, Emancipation, and Equality

THE AMERICAN CIVIL WAR broke out in the spring of 1861. As soon as the news reached Harriet Tubman in Canada, she left to join the fight. The United States, or Union, army didn't accept black men as soldiers early on in the war—and it certainly did not accept black women. But Harriet was well known among abolitionist politicians, including Governor John Andrew of Massachusetts, who helped her get a posting in South Carolina. There she went to work helping slaves who'd escaped to safety behind Union lines. Among Harriet's many other skills was a talent for nursing. The Union army supplied her makeshift hospitals with few medicines. But Harriet had a keen knowledge of local medicinal plants and folk remedies, and she used those to heal escaped slaves and soldiers. Many welcomed the care and healing powers of Moses herself.

Harriet Tubman was a woman of action. She grew frustrated with President Lincoln's unwillingness to let blacks be soldiers, as well as his reluctance to free the slaves. "He can [win the war] by setting the Negroes free," she complained. When Lincoln did allow black men to join the Union army in 1863, Harriet Tubman recruited many soldiers. She was also assigned the job of collecting information that would help the Union army defeat its enemy, the Confederate army of the South. Harriet enlisted seven former slaves and two black riverboat pilots as fellow spies and scouts. Harriet and her spies traveled the area, collecting information about Confederate ammunition stores, food sources, and troop movements. As a black woman, Harriet could more easily move about the countryside unchallenged. Few suspected that "an old slave woman" could be a Union spy! She also had the trust of slaves who were still on plantations. Many slave owners told their slaves that Union soldiers were monsters who would kill their children. For this reason, most slaves wouldn't risk talking to a white Union soldier. But these same slaves would gladly tell Moses what they knew.

Information collected by the spies and scouts under Harriet Tubman's command soon led to a daring raid. Tubman helped lead three Union gunboats up South Carolina's Combahee River, freeing the slaves of the plantations they passed. More than 750 slaves were taken aboard the gunboats. Harriet described how the slaves came running toward the boats with children, pigs, and chickens in tow. "I never see such a sight," said Harriet. The Combahee raid made Harriet a full-fledged soldier, and she

began dressing like one. Her uniform was a dark "Federal" blue coat and dress. But she proudly wore pant-like bloomers during raids. As a soldier, Harriet carried a musket, a canteen, and a first aid kit.

The Civil War was filled with horrors, and Harriet witnessed her share of them. She helped bury the casualties among the 1,500 dead and wounded white and black soldiers after the Union's defeat at Fort Wagner at Morris Island, South Carolina. She described the horrible battle to a historian this way: "And then we saw the lightning, and that was the guns; and then we heard the thunder, and that was the big guns; and then we heard the rain falling, and that was the blood falling; and when we came to get in the crops, it was dead men that we reaped."

Breaking the Balance

What started the American Civil War? Why did the North and South split apart? What could possibly make neighbors and families take sides against each other and become enemies? The short answer is slavery.

The South's plantations and way of life depended on the forced labor of African Americans. The slave states of the South wanted to keep it that way. Most Southerners accepted slavery as part of their economy. And many Southerners defended slavery with beliefs that blacks were inferior to whites. The free states of the North had a different kind of economy. It was the more modern part of the country, with growing mill and factory towns. The North prospered without slaves, and many Northerners believed that slavery was wrong. These basic differences between the North and South were why Abraham Lincoln called America "a house divided."

A house divided against itself cannot stand. I believe this government cannot endure permanently half slave and half free. I do not expect the Union to be dissolved—I do not expect the house to fall—but I do expect it will cease to be divided. It will become all one thing, or all the other. Either the opponents of slavery will arrest the further spread of it, and place it where the public mind shall rest in the belief that it is in the course of ultimate extinction; or its advocates will push it forward till it shall become alike lawful in all the States, old as well as new, North as well as South.

ABRAHAM LINCOLN speaking as a (defeated) U.S. Senate candidate from Illinois in 1858

The United States government wanted to keep both halves of its "divided house" happy. The federal government had been trying to balance the power of the North and the South ever since the nation began. Compromises of power between the North and the South started in the U.S. Constitution. The historic document called for an end to the importation of Africans by 1808. But it also allowed each slave to be counted as three-fifths of a free person for the purpose of representation in the U.S. Congress, which boosted Southern political power. When Maine was admitted into the United States as a free state in 1820, Missouri was allowed to enter as a slave state to keep the balance even—12 free states and 12 slave states.

When California became a state in 1850, it didn't want to allow slavery. But Southern U.S. Congressmen knew that a free California would mean that free states would outnumber slave states. They wouldn't vote for it. So Congress passed a set of laws called the Compromise of 1850. California would be a free state, but the Compromise of 1850 gave proslavery states something they wanted. The new western territories would be allowed to decide for themselves whether or not they wanted slavery. Selling slaves in Washington, D.C., became illegal, but slave owners got something else they badly wanted—a tough fugitive slave law (see page 57).

Riots and Raids

The Compromise of 1850 didn't satisfy either side for very long. Slavery supporters immediately began to spread slavery into the western territories. And the Fugitive Slave Law turned slavery opponents into abolition activists and Underground Railroad workers. One militant Underground Railroad stationmaster was the former slave William Parker (see page 135). In 1851 Parker lived in Christiana, Pennsylvania, not far from the Maryland border. Free blacks and fugitive slaves in this part of Pennsylvania were terrorized by the Gap Gang, a group of kidnappers and bounty hunters who were always looking for runaways to turn in for reward money. The Gap Gang was known to kidnap free blacks to sell into slavery as well.

William Parker was a leader of the local black vigilance committee and an Underground Railroad worker. Parker and Frederick Douglass had known each other as slaves in Maryland. Parker had heard Douglass's speech that warned blacks to protect themselves against kidnappers now that the Fugitive Slave Act was law. Parker had no intention of letting bounty hunters capture or kidnap anyone on his watch.

THE EVENTS AT WILLIAM PARKER'S HOUSE BECAME KNOWN AS THE CHRISTIANA RIOT.

Kidnapping was so common . . . that we were kept in constant fear. We would hear of slaveholders or kidnappers every two or three weeks; sometimes a party of white men would break into a house and take a man away, no one knew where; and, again, a whole family would be carried off. There was no power to protect them, nor prevent it. So completely roused were my feelings, that I vowed to let no slaveholder take back a fugitive, if I could but get my eye on him.

WILLIAM PARKER, an Underground Railroad agent and stationmaster

On the morning of September 11, 1851, four fugitives were hiding in Parker's house. George and Joshua Hammond, Noah Buley, and Nelson Ford had run away from their Maryland plantation. A member of the Gap Gang had told their owner, Edward Gorsuch, where the fugitives were hiding. Gorsuch, his son Dickinson, and a posse of men that included a federal marshal went to Parker's house. They demanded that Parker turn over the runaways. While the men argued and threatened each other downstairs, Parker's wife, Eliza, sounded the alarm. Eliza Parker managed to blow a horn from a second-story window even while the posse shot at her. Soon armed black and white townspeople showed up, and the Christiana Riot started. An hour later, Edward Gorsuch lay dead in front of William Parker's house in a pool of blood.

President Millard Fillmore sent in 45 U.S. Marines and 40 Philadelphia policemen to round up suspects. But Parker and his men were already on their way to Canada. The 38 people arrested in Pennsylvania were tried for resisting the Fugitive Slave Law and for treason against the United States. Not a single person was convicted—all of them were set free. The Christiana Riot further fueled the growing anger between the North and South during the 1850s. So did the book *Uncle Tom's Cabin* (see page 42), the Dred Scott decision (see page 15), and the Kansas–Nebraska Act of 1854. The Act

allowed the people of the Kansas and Nebraska territories to decide whether to become slave or free states. It quickly caused violence to break out between proslavers and abolitionists in these territories. Towns were burned and settlers were murdered along the Kansas–Missouri border. This so-called Bleeding Kansas conflict

HERO OF FREEDOM

WILLIAM PARKER

(1822–?)

WILLIAM PARKER was born a slave in Maryland. He was a field hand on a plantation of seventy slaves. Parker learned to fight early on in life. As a boy, he had to fight to get a warm spot by the fire. As a youth, his master arranged prize fights for him. "My Rights at the fireplace were won by my child-fists; my rights as a freeman were, under God, secured by my own right arm," he wrote.

Parker and his brothers fled the plantation after a young friend was sold away. They reached Baltimore, Maryland, on foot and disguised themselves as local workers by covering their clothes in brick dust. They moved on to the free state of Pennsylvania, where they settled. The kidnapping and recapture of former slaves and free blacks was common in the area. Parker soon became active in a secret vigilance committee of refugees who vowed to prevent the recapture of fugitives. Parker saved a number of fugitives from recapture and was shot in the ankle during one of the rescue missions.

After the Christiana Riot (see page 134), William Parker escaped to Canada. He and his family reunited and eventually moved to the settlement of former slaves in Elgin, Canada (see page 124).

showed that Americans would fight over slavery. It also gave rise to John Brown.

John Brown was a militant abolitionist who believed in fighting—and killing—for the antislavery cause. Brown and five of his sons went to the Kansas Territory, taking a wagon of weapons with them. They were soon leading the antislavery Free Soil militia there. Three nights after a proslavery mob burned and looted the town of Lawrence, Kansas, in May 1856, John Brown took revenge. Brown, his sons, and two other men went looking for proslavery settlers. They dragged five men out of their cabins and hacked each of them to death.

Like many abolitionists, Brown no longer believed that the U.S. government would end slavery. John Brown was convinced that slaves needed to be armed and led in a revolt. In 1859 Brown and a band of 21 armed men (including five free blacks) seized the federal arsenal at Harpers Ferry, Virginia. They planned to arm slaves with the arsenal's stored weapons. But Brown's men were quickly trapped. U.S. military troops killed half of them—including two of Brown's sons—and captured the rest. John Brown was tried for treason and hanged. Many Northerners and African Americans saw Brown as a martyred saint who gave his life to end slavery. Many Southerners saw Brown as one more reason why slave states should no longer be part of the United States of America, but should instead form their own separate country.

THE U.S. MARINES STORMED THE ARSENAL AT HARPERS FERRY AND QUICKLY PUT AN END TO THE RAID LED BY JOHN BROWN.

❖❖ *Dear Father, Mother, Brothers Henry, William and Freddy and Sisters Sarah and Mary:*
I will take my pen, for the last time, to write you who are bound to me by those strong ties . . .

I am well, both in body and in mind. And now, dear ones, if it were not that I knew your hearts will be filled with sorrow at my fate, I could pass from this earth without a regret . . . I fully believe that not only myself, but also all three of my poor comrades who are to ascend the same scaffold—(a scaffold already made sacred to the cause of freedom by the death of that great champion of human freedom—Captain John Brown) are prepared to meet our God . . . in the end, though we meet no more on earth, we shall meet in heaven, where we shall not be parted by the demands of the cruel and unjust monster Slavery.

▨ JOHN A. COPELAND, a free black who was hanged for participating in the raid on Harpers Ferry

A Broken Nation Takes Sides

Americans elected their 16th president in the fall of 1860. As a candidate, Abraham Lincoln had promised to keep slavery out of the new western territories. Southerners feared that Lincoln would eventually end slavery in the South, too. In December 1860, following Lincoln's election, the state of South Carolina withdrew, or "seceded," from the United States. By the time Lincoln was sworn in as president in March 1861, six more South-

HERO OF FREEDOM
JOHN BROWN
(1800–1859)

JOHN BROWN was born in Connecticut. His family was deeply religious, and Brown carried a fierce sense of right and wrong into adulthood. In 1849 Brown settled his family in New York State, in a community where a number of fugitive slaves lived. Brown worked as an Underground Railroad stationmaster, and his abolitionist views grew stronger and more militant.

In 1855 Brown followed five of his sons to the Kansas Territory. They went to defend the antislavery Free Soil settlers who were under attack from proslavery Missouri raiders. The massacre that John Brown led in May (see page 136) gave rise to even more murders and violence in the "Bleeding Kansas" conflict. But Brown was never arrested for the massacre. He claimed that God ordered the murders.

Brown toured the abolitionist meetings of the Northeast to collect money for his planned slave revolt. Many agreed with his militant opposition to slavery. Harriet Tubman supposedly helped John Brown recruit soldiers for his raid on Harpers Ferry. Brown called her "General Tubman." It is said that Tubman regarded Brown, not Abraham Lincoln, as the true emancipator of her people. John Brown's raid at Harpers Ferry failed. But his trial for treason gave Brown the chance to speak out against slavery and again claim that he was following God's orders. John Brown died a martyred saint and hero to many Americans.

ern states had seceded. Together with South Carolina, they formed the Confederate States of America. They wrote their own constitution.

It guaranteed all Confederate states the right to "the institution of negro slavery" in the "States or Territories of the Confederate States." Jefferson Davis was elected their president.

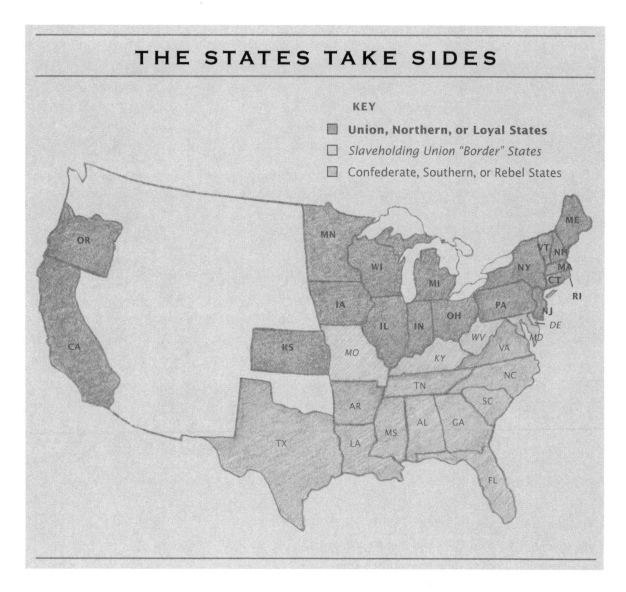

THE STATES TAKE SIDES

KEY

■ **Union, Northern, or Loyal States**

□ *Slaveholding Union "Border" States*

▨ Confederate, Southern, or Rebel States

❖❖ Our new Government . . . its foundations are laid, its cornerstone rests, upon the great truth that the negro is not equal to the white man; that slavery, subordination to the superior race, is his natural and moral condition. This, our new Government, is the first, in the history of the world, based upon this great physical, philosophical, and moral truth.

▨ ALEXANDER H. STEPHENS, vice president of the Confederacy

On April 12, 1861, Confederate forces began firing on Fort Sumter in Charleston, South Carolina. The Confederates considered South Carolina to be part of their country—not the United States. The United States military fort and its Union soldiers were no longer welcome. Confederate fighters forced the U.S. soldiers to surrender Fort Sumter. President Lincoln sent in Union troops to take back the fort. The American Civil War had begun. Both sides started organizing armies and enlisting soldiers.

Eleven Southern slave states fought on the Confederate, or Rebel, side—South Carolina, North Carolina, Mississippi, Florida, Alabama, Georgia, Louisiana, Texas, Tennessee, Virginia, and Arkansas. Twenty-three states fought for the Union, or Yankee, side, including four slave states—Delaware, Maryland, Kentucky, and Missouri. The western part of Virginia formed a new state, West Virginia, and it also fought with the Union. These slaveholding "border" states, which were loyal to the Union, saw some the heaviest fighting in the war. Some men from the border states joined the Confederate army and ended up fighting neighbors, brothers, cousins, and old classmates.

It wasn't an even fight. The Union states were home to more than twice as many people as the Confederate states. In addition, one-third of the nine million people living in the Confederacy were slaves. Besides having more soldiers, the North had many more factories and a large navy. But the fighting and battles went on for four long, bloody years. By the time it was over, 620,000 soldiers had died. The Civil War took more American lives than any other war—before or since.

CIVIL WAR ENACTMENTS ARE A POPULAR PASTIME EVEN TODAY, MORE THAN 140 YEARS AFTER THE "WAR BETWEEN THE STATES" BEGAN.

Human Contraband

War often brings chaos. Many slaves were able to take advantage of the wartime turmoil and flee their masters. Union soldiers came upon many runaway slaves as they marched south. What should be done about them? The Union declared the slaves illegal goods, or "contraband," that should be taken from the Rebels. In the case of slaves, the contraband was to be set free. Slaves were soon fleeing into Union camps by the hundreds. A few were given land to live on. Others lived in contraband camps, which were too often full of disease and hunger. Thousands went to work for the Union army as laborers, cooks, nurses, and scouts. Enslaved African Americans behind Union lines were getting their freedom. Black and abolitionist leaders such as Frederick Douglass saw the chance for something glorious to come out of the gruesome war—emancipation for the slaves. Would Lincoln do it? Would he free the slaves?

The Yankee soldiers landed at Paducah, Kentucky. I went down to see them once in a while. My master thought I was going to run away and stay with the Yankee soldiers. A crowd of the slaveholders came and bound me with ropes and carried me down to the blacksmith shop, and put a shackle around my ankle and a six foot chain fastened to it . . . I broke the chain and escaped. I had twenty-seven miles to go to Paducah, Kentucky, to get to the Union soldiers. The next morning by sunrise, I was in Paducah. When I got there, I went to General Wallace and Captain Lyman, and they asked me if I could cook. I said yes. I still had the iron shackle on my leg. They carried me down to the blacksmith's and had the shackle filed off. Captain Lyman told me he thought I was very ambitious to file that chain and escape. He said he would keep me as long as I would stay with him . . . In about three days my master came there after me . . . He said, you have a boy in here I want. The General questioned him very close. The General asked him what I had done to have such iron shackles on my leg. He told him I had not done anything. General Wallace told him he guessed he would keep me, and told him never to come back after me any more, for if he did he would arrest him.

WILLIAM WEBB, a former slave in Mississippi and Kentucky

Abraham Lincoln wanted to keep the United States—North and South—together as one country. Lincoln believed that slavery was wrong, and he wanted to see it die out. But he was fighting the Civil War to preserve the Union, not necessarily to free the slaves. However, the two goals became one and the same in late 1862, when Abraham Lincoln issued the Emancipation Proclamation. It said that if the Confederate states didn't rejoin the Union before January 1, their slaves would be free. No state left the Confederacy. On January 1, 1863,

THESE VIRGINIA "CONTRABAND" SLAVES ARE BEHIND UNION LINES IN VIRGINIA DURING THE SUMMER OF 1862.

all the slaves in the Rebel states were declared free. The War between the States had became a war to free the slaves.

◆◇◆ *I, Abraham Lincoln, President of the United States . . . on this 1st day of January, A.D. 1863 . . . And by virtue of the power and for the purpose aforesaid, I do order and declare that all persons held as slaves within said designated States and parts of States are, and henceforward shall be, free.*

▨ ABRAHAM LINCOLN, in his Emancipation Proclamation

Lincoln's Emancipation Proclamation didn't immediately end slavery in America. Rebel states didn't obey the proclamation and free their slaves. The Confederates didn't consider themselves bound by U.S. laws and proclamations because they didn't consider Lincoln their president or the United States their country. As Union soldiers marched south through Rebel territory and reclaimed it for the United States, they had to free the slaves that were behind their lines. However, the Emancipation Proclamation only freed slaves in Rebel states. It did not free the one million slaves living in Union slave states. Lincoln didn't free the Union slaves because he feared it would cause those border states to go over to the Confederate side. As a

AFRICAN AMERICANS WERE PUT TO WORK RIGHT AWAY AS COOKS AND LABORERS FOR THE UNION ARMY, BUT THEY WEREN'T ALLOWED TO FIGHT FOR THE UNION UNTIL 1863.

result, a Union officer from Kentucky might help free slaves in the conquered South while still owning slaves at home. A great many slaves would have to wait until the war was over for their freedom.

THE EMANCIPATION PROCLAMATION MADE THE CIVIL WAR A FIGHT TO FREE SLAVES, LIKE THESE LIVING ON A SOUTH CAROLINA PLANTATION.

AFTER THE EMANCIPATION PROCLAMATION, THE UNION ARMY FREED SLAVES AS THEY MARCHED THROUGH REBEL TERRITORY.

Black Soldiers and Sailors

Many Northern free blacks rushed to join the Union army in 1861 after the battle at Fort Sumter. But they were turned away and told, "This is a white man's war." Not accepting black soldiers was part of Lincoln's efforts to keep the border states on the Union side. But after two hard years of fighting, the Union needed more soldiers—white or black. The Emancipation Proclamation included a section that finally allowed black men to join the bat-

tle. Many African American leaders helped recruit former slaves and free blacks to join Union forces. Frederick Douglass quickly put his famous speaking skills to work encouraging black men to fight for the Union. Underground Railroad conductor John Parker, abolitionist and stationmaster William Wells Brown, and Mary Ann Shadd Cary helped recruit black soldiers, too.

 *Men of Color, To Arms! . . . Liberty won by white men would lose half its luster. "Who would*

be free themselves must strike the blow." "Better even die free, than to live slaves." This is the sentiment of every brave colored man amongst us . . . By every consideration which binds you to your enslaved fellow . . . by every aspiration which you cherish for the freedom and equality of yourselves and your children . . . I urge you to fly to arms, and smite with death the power that would bury the government and your liberty in the same hopeless grave . . . This is our golden opportunity . . . Let us win for ourselves the gratitude of our country, and the best blessings of our posterity through all time.

⊞ FREDERICK DOUGLASS, an abolitionist, African American leader, and former slave

African American men quickly answered the call to arms. They were placed in segregated all-black regiments formed by the War Department's Bureau of Colored Troops. Many whites doubted that runaway slaves and free blacks could be good soldiers. But the critics were proved wrong. Black regiments distinguished themselves early on in a number of famous battles, including those at Fort Wagner and Fort Pillow, as well as in the Battle of New Market Heights. After a particularly bloody clash in what is today Oklahoma, at Honey Springs, Union General James G. Blunt wrote: "I never saw such fighting as was done by the Negro regiment . . . The question that negroes will fight is settled; besides they make better solders in every respect than any troops I have ever had under my command."

Free blacks, fugitive slaves living in the North and in Canada, and newly freed "contrabands" behind Union lines signed up to fight for Lincoln's army and navy. More than three-quarters of them had once been slaves. One such former slave was Elijah P. Marrs. Like many black Union soldiers, he'd fled his master to enlist. Life for black soldiers like Marrs was difficult. Besides facing the horror of battle, the soldiers lived under poor conditions. Marrs and his men often had to steal food to feed themselves. They marched as many as 20 miles in a day and slept in snow and holes dug in the ground. Sickness killed half of the soldiers who died in the Civil War, and Marrs himself was often ill. Black soldiers were paid less than white soldiers and were given poorer weapons, fewer supplies, and less medical care. About one-third of all African Americans in the military during the Civil War died.

⊗ I was twenty-one years of age. The war between the North and South was upon us, and ideas of freedom began to steal across my brain . . . I remember the morning I made up my mind to join the United States Army. I started to Simpsonville, and walking along I met many of my old comrades . . . I told them of my determination,

CIVIL WAR IN YOUR STATE

MOST OF THE FAMOUS Civil War battles happened in southeastern states such as Virginia and Tennessee. But there were Civil War battles as far west as places that are today Idaho and New Mexico, and as far north as North Dakota. The War between the States affected the whole country—including the territories that weren't yet states.

Discover how the American Civil War affected the region where you live. If you have access to the Internet, start with the American Civil War Web site listed on page 159. It includes a link to a list of battle sites by state. Another way to find out about Civil War history in your area is to call or write to your town's, city's, or county's historical society or visitors bureau. Many public libraries can also help you track down local Civil War information.

THE SOLDIERS OF COMPANY E, FOURTH U.S. COLORED INFANTRY, WERE PART OF THE UNION ARMY'S DEFENSES OF WASHINGTON, D.C., AT FORT LINCOLN.

Company L, Twelfth U. S. Colored Artillery. The Orderly Sergeant called the roll, and when he called "Marrs, Elijah," I promptly answered . . . said I, "this is better than slavery, though I do march in line to the tap of the drum." I felt freedom in my bones, and when I saw the American eagle, with outspread wings, upon the American flag . . . the thought came to me, "Give me liberty or give me death." Then all fear banished. I had quit thinking as a child and had commenced to think as a man.

☒ Elijah P. Marrs, a former Kentucky slave who escaped and joined the Union army

Eventually, about 180,000 African Americans served in 163 Union army units during the Civil War. Another 33,000 served in the Union navy. One of those sailors brought his own battleship when he signed up! His name was Robert Smalls. Smalls was a slave in South Carolina and a skilled steamboat wheelman. His master hired him out as the pilot on a cotton transport steamship called the *Planter.* Many slaves who lived in Confederate states during the Civil War were forced to work for the Rebels. Most slaves were drafted as laborers, cooks, and servants. After the war started, the Confederate navy seized the *Planter,* turned it into a gunboat, and forced Smalls to pilot it. Robert Smalls and the other slaves who were

and asked all who desired to join my company . . . and in one half hour we were within the lines of the Union Army, and by eight o'clock we were at the recruiting office in the city of Louisville . . . By twelve o'clock the owner of every man of us was in the city hunting his slaves, but we had all enlisted . . . I enlisted on the 26th day of September, 1864, and was immediately . . . assigned to

forced to work on the *Planter* soon decided they'd had enough.

Early on the morning of May 13, 1862, Smalls and the other slaves snuck their families onboard the *Planter*. They raised the Confederate flag on the gunboat and headed out into Charleston Harbor. As they neared the Union navy's blockade in the harbor, Smalls replaced the Confederate flag with a white flag. Rebel gunboats opened fire, but it was too late. Smalls and the 12 other slaves aboard the *Planter* were safe in Union territory. The *Planter* became a Union gunboat, and Robert Smalls (see right) became its free black navy captain. Captain Smalls fought in 17 battles at the helm of the *Planter* during the Civil War.

Agents, Conductors, and Brakemen During the War

Many Underground Railroad agents, conductors, brakemen, and stationmasters continued their efforts during the Civil War. Some joined the Union army or navy. People such as Harriet Tubman and others who knew the countryside made valuable spies and scouts. Many of the stationmasters and agents who'd cared for fleeing runaways before the war aided them during the war as well. Thousands of

slaves fled their masters and took refuge behind Union lines during the fighting. Most of these runaways had no money or possessions, and

HERO OF FREEDOM

ROBERT SMALLS

(1839–1915)

ROBERT SMALLS was born to plantation slave parents. At 12 years of age, Smalls was taken away from his family. His master took him to Charleston, South Carolina, and hired him out. Smalls worked as a hotel waiter, a carriage driver, and a boat rigger before becoming a steamboat pilot, or "wheelman." He was the pilot of the steamship the *Planter* when it was seized by the Confederate navy and turned into a gunboat. Smalls was forced to pilot it.

On May 13, 1862, Robert Smalls and 12 other slaves aboard the *Planter* took over the steamship. Smalls piloted the boat into Charleston Harbor and turned it over to the Union navy. Thanks to Smalls, the Union navy got a gunboat, its four cannons, and intelligence on the Confederate's defenses. Robert Smalls got his freedom, and he became famous for the daring escape. He even met President Lincoln.

After the Civil War ended, Smalls went back to the South and bought his former master's home—including the slave quarters where he was born. Smalls served in the South Carolina House of Representatives and in the Senate from 1868 to 1874. He was elected to the U.S. Congress in 1875.

WARTIME WRAPPINGS

AMONG HARRIET TUBMAN'S many talents was her skill as a healer. While serving in the Union army during the Civil War she carried a first aid kit. Tubman often worked in makeshift camp hospitals, nursing both white and black soldiers as well as fugitive slaves who'd fled behind Union lines. Tubman not only knew how to care for wounds and broken bones. She knew how to use local plants to treat dysentery and other maladies. Try your own hand at field bandaging in this activity.

You'll need a triangular bandage and a friend to practice on. You can buy a real triangular bandage at a drugstore or an army surplus store. Or just make one. Simply cut an old sheet or shirt into a square yard. Then cut from one corner of the square to its opposite to make two triangular bandages.

1. To make an arm sling, sandwich the bandage between the bent arm and the torso. Then bring the lower end of the triangle up over the arm to meet the other end and tie it at the neck. You can secure the elbow end with either a safety pin or a knot to keep the arm from slipping.

2. To cover the head, wrap the widest part of the bandage around the forehead. Then cross the ends at the back and bring them back around to the front and tie them.

3. To cover an injured knee, lay the triangular bandage over the knee so that its widest corner points up toward the thigh. Then fold up the bottom of the bandage, wrap its ends around the back of the knee and tie it over the top of the knee. Bring the remaining corner down over the tied corners and tuck it under the folded front.

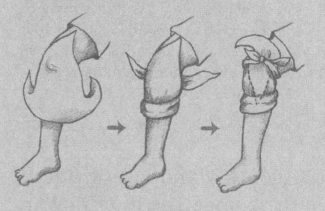

they had just abandoned the only home they'd ever known. Refugee and contraband camps were often miserable places that teemed with diseases. There was often not enough food to feed all of their inhabitants. Organizations such as the National Freedman's Relief Association and religious groups tried to meet some of the needs of newly freed slaves.

&❧& *When the civil war in America broke out, somehow the coloured people in Canada had an idea that the result of it would be the abolition of slavery. If I could have carried a gun, I would have gone personally, but I thought it was my duty to talk to the people. I told them "that the young and able-bodied ought to go into the field like men, that they should stand up to the rack, and help the government." My oldest son, Tom, who was in California, enlisted on a man-of-war in San Francisco, and I suppose he must have been killed, as I have not heard from him since that time.*

▨ JOSIAH HENSON, an Underground Railroad conductor and brakeman who escaped slavery and lived in Canada

Slaves who still lived in Confederate-held territory had it rough, too. Many were taken from their families and forced to work as laborers, cooks, and servants for the Confederate forces. Others were sent into battle as personal servants of their masters. As the war dragged on, everyday life became difficult for many Southerners. Property was destroyed, men were off fighting, and crops weren't selling. Many slaveowners fell on tough times and could barely provide for themselves, much less their slaves. Slaves resisted their owners more and more as the war went on. So many slaves were running off or disobeying their masters that the Confederacy declared that owners of 20 or more slaves couldn't be drafted. They were to stay home and control their slaves.

&❧& *My master's eldest son volunteered for service, and I was sent into the Army to be with him, and to cook and do other things. I had an opportunity of seeing much of the campaign around York town . . . During the second year of the War, [my master] Mr. Brent died . . . After his death I had to be at home most of the time until the close of the war. During some of this time the widow hired me out to a firm to make cigars. She received twenty dollars a week for my services.*

▨ THOMAS L. JOHNSON, a former Virginia slave

&❧& *When de war started 'mos' all I know 'bout it was all de white mens go to Montgomery an' jine de army . . . Dey 'lected Mista Jeff Davis president*

*an' done busted de Nunited States wide open . . .
Atter dat dar warn't much happen on de plantation 'cep'in' gangs of so'jers passin' th'ough gwine
off to de war. Den 'bout ebry so often a squad of
Confederate so'jers would come to de neighborhood gatherin' up rations for Gin'ral Lee's army
dey say. Dat make it purty hard on bofe whites an'
blacks, takin' off some of de bes' stock an' runnin'
us low on grub.*

▧ WALTER CALLOWAY, a former Alabama slave

In March 1864 President Lincoln gave General Ulysses S. Grant supreme command of the
army. The Union had more soldiers and more
supplies than the Confederacy. Grant knew this,
and he put his men to work wearing down the
Rebels. Grant's army slowly closed in around
Confederate General Robert E. Lee's forces in
Virginia. Meanwhile, Union General William
Tecumseh Sherman captured Atlanta and
burned it. Then he led his men on a 300-mile
(480-kilometer) march to Savannah, Georgia.
The soldiers destroyed much of what they
passed by in an attempt to break the South's will
to keep fighting. By March 1865 General Lee's
Confederate army in Virginia had few men left,
and even fewer supplies. General Grant and his
Union army soon captured Richmond, the
Capitol of the Confederacy. On April 9, 1865,
the two generals met at a farmhouse in Appo-
mattox Court House, Virginia. Outfitted in a
spotless dress uniform, Confederate General
Robert E. Lee surrendered to General Grant.
The American Civil War was finally over.

✦✦ *On Sunday, April 2nd, 1865, there was great
excitement in the city, "General Grant . . . was
closing in around us." . . . In the afternoon many
of the families began to leave the city, and late in
the evening President Davis, General S. S. Cooper,
General Lee, and staff all left Richmond . . . At the
break of day a coloured man was the first to carry
the news . . . that President Davis and General Lee
had "skedaddled." At eight o'clock in the morning
about forty of the United States Cavalry . . . rode
into Richmond, and proceeded at once to the public square of the capital . . . Soon the Stars and
Stripes were seen floating over the old State
Capital.*

*The joy and rejoicing of the coloured peo-
ple . . . defies description. For days the manifesta-
tions of delight were displayed in many ways. The
places of worship were kept open, and hundreds
met for prayer and praise . . . I cannot now
describe the joy of my soul at that time . . . No
longer was I a mere chattel, but a man, free in
body, free in soul; praise the Lord. It is impossible
to give an adequate idea of the abounding joy of
the people—the great multitude of liberated
slaves—after the long years of toil and suffering . . . The long night of affliction in the house of*

our bondage had passed, and that deeply desired and hoped for and prayed for time had come!

⊞ Thomas L. Johnson, a former Virginia slave

Freedom and Tragedy

Two hundred and fifty years of legal slavery ended with the Civil War. The Thirteenth Amendment to the U.S. Constitution made it official: "Neither slavery nor involuntary servitude . . . shall exist within the United States." Four million enslaved African Americans were now free.

⬦ *My boss called us out in the yard under a tree one afternoon. He had a newspaper in his hand. He read from it and then told us it was the Emancipation Proclamation issued at Washington by President Lincoln. We didn't quite understand what it was all about until he informed us that it meant we were slaves no longer, that we were free to go as we liked, to work for anyone who would hire us and be responsible to no one but ourselves.*

⊞ Andrew Evans, a former Missouri slave

The Union's victory in the Civil War meant that the United States remained one country. That was President Abraham Lincoln's goal all

HERO OF FREEDOM

ABRAHAM LINCOLN
(1809–1865)

ABRAHAM LINCOLN was born to nearly illiterate pioneer parents. He grew up poor on Kentucky, Indiana, and Illinois farms, and he had little schooling. As a young man he tried his hand at many jobs, and was a rail-splitter, a flatboatman, a storekeeper, a postmaster, and a surveyor. Lincoln eventually decided to study law. He educated himself and became a successful lawyer. By the time he entered politics, Lincoln was known for his intelligence and honesty.

Lincoln served in the Illinois State Legislature from 1834 to 1840 and in the U.S. Congress from 1847 to 1849. During his years as a legislator, Lincoln formed his ideas about slavery. In a letter to a friend, Lincoln wrote about a steamboat trip they'd taken on the Ohio River. "You may remember, as I well do, that from Louisville [Kentucky] to the mouth of the Ohio there were, on board, ten or a dozen slaves, shackled together with irons. That sight was a continual torment to me; and I see something like it every time I touch the Ohio, or any other slave-border." But while Lincoln didn't like slavery, he wasn't an abolitionist. As long as the new territories didn't become slave states, Lincoln believed that slavery would gradually die out on its own in all of America.

Lincoln's opposition to slavery in the territories got him elected president in 1860. It also caused Southern slave states to withdraw from the Union. Once Lincoln presented his Emancipation Proclamation, the Civil War became a war to free the slaves, as well as to preserve the Union. For this, Abraham Lincoln became known as the Great Emancipator.

JUNETEENTH

JUNETEENTH is an African American celebration of the ending of slavery held every year on June 19. Juneteenth celebrates the day in 1865 when the Union army entered Galveston, Texas, and ordered that all the slaves in the state be freed.

When Union soldiers marched into Texas that June day, the Civil War had been over for two months and the slaves had been freed by Lincoln's Emancipation Proclamation more than two years earlier. But slave owners in Texas had kept the news from their slaves.

The Juneteenth holiday started in Texas in the years following the Civil War, and it soon spread to other states. Today it's a yearly celebration of freedom and African American culture. Many Juneteenth celebrations include music, food, games, and picnics. Use what you've learned about the struggle for freedom to plan your own Juneteenth celebration. You can include other activities from this book, such as making Adinkra cloth (see page 4), playing banjo music (see page 26), singing freedom songs (see page 56), and telling family stories (see page 24), as well as games, a trivia contest, and food.

MANY CALLED ABRAHAM LINCOLN THE GREAT EMANCIPATOR.

along. Tragically, Lincoln had little time to enjoy the fact that he'd preserved the Union. Only five days after Lee's surrender, the unthinkable happened. The Great Emancipator was killed. Abraham Lincoln, the man who freed the slaves and saved the Union, was murdered on April 14, 1865, by John Wilkes Booth, a proslavery Confederate. Booth shouted, "The South is avenged!" after fatally shooting the president in the head.

The assassination of Lincoln brought home a tough truth to Americans: Not everyone was happy to be back in the Union. Much of the South was in ruins after the war, and many Southerners were bitter. The Fourteenth Amendment granted African Americans citizenship in 1868. And the Fifteenth Amendment gave voting rights to black men in 1870 (no woman would be allowed to vote until 1920). But many former slave owners would never accept their former slaves as citizens. And racist groups such as the Ku Klux Klan terrorized blacks and did all they could to deny African Americans their rights.

◆◆◆ *I was a perfect curiosity to the white people of Simpsonville, [Kentucky,] simply because I was the first colored school-teacher they had ever seen, and yet I was no stranger to them, for just three years from the time I left Simpsonville, a slave, to join the United States Army, I returned a free man and a school teacher. They would come to visit me and stare, and wonder at the change, and this was especially the case with my original owners . . . They would send me sums to solve, such as 146+12-19+200, and the like, to see if I really knew anything. Then when I would work them out they would say to my colored friends, "That Elijah is a smart nigger!"*

One day, while the school children were at play, during recess, some one fired a shot among them. I saw the man who did the shooting, and going to him, charged him with the offense. He denied it, and raised a club to strike me, when I retreated to the school-room, glad to get away alive, for, though the war was over, the K. K. K. was in full blast, and no man was safe from their depredations.

⊞ ELIJAH MARRS, a former Kentucky slave who escaped slavery to fight for the Union

Day-to-day life was difficult for newly freed slaves. Many were now homeless and penniless. The Freedman's Bureau set up hospitals and schools for blacks, and the federal bureau resettled thousands of former slaves. Many freed slaves moved north to start new lives in freedom. Thousands moved out west. African Americans helped build railroads, worked as cowboys, and were pioneer settlers, too. But many poor blacks ended up having to live and work on the farms where they'd once been slaves.

⬦ *[B]ut now I had a new problem to solve, which was to support and clothe myself and a wife and pay doctors' bills, which was something new to me. I had never been trained in the school of economy, where I could learn the art of self-support, as my master had always attended to that little matter from my earliest recollections . . .*

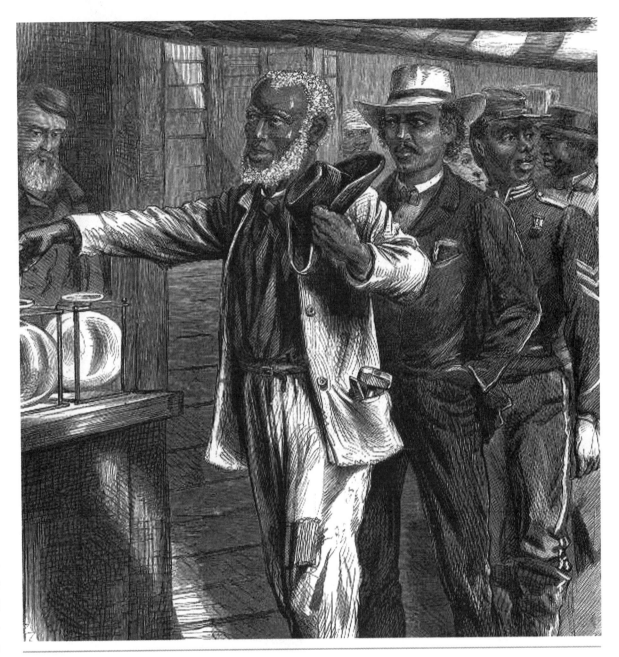

BLACK MEN WHO'D LIVED THEIR ENTIRE LIVES IN THE UNITED STATES VOTED FOR THE FIRST TIME IN 1870.

MANY PLACES WHERE THE UNDERGROUND RAILROAD ONCE RAN ARE NOW SLEEPY HAMLETS WITH ONLY PLAQUES AND OLD BUILDINGS LEFT TO REMIND VISITORS OF THE FEARLESS CONDUCTORS, BRAVE STATIONMASTERS, AND COURAGEOUS RUNAWAYS THAT ONCE STIRRED UP TROUBLE IN THEIR TOWNS.

I had lived to be twenty-eight years old, and had never been placed in a position where I had occasion to give this matter a single thought . . . although I had been trained to work from a child . . . with a will and ability to perform hard manual labor, yet I had not learned the art of spending my earnings to the best advantage . . . This was the condition of the Colored people at the close of the war. They were set free without a dollar, without a foot of land, and without the wherewithal to get the next meal even . . . These slaves had been trained to do hard manual labor from the time that they were large enough to perform it, to the end of their lives, right along, and received no education or instruction in the way of economy.

▨ Henry Clay Bruce, a former Missouri slave

As difficult as life was for African Americans after the Civil War, they were finally a free people. They'd gained freedom from slavery, the right to vote, and full citizenship. Many former slaves who had once risked everything to escape to freedom could now return home. Mothers greeted long-lost sons, and yearned-for fathers were reunited with their children.

Thousands of the black fugitives who had settled in Canada moved back to the United States. Many had traveled to Canada via the Underground Railroad. But now it was no longer needed. The Underground Railroad shut down. The African Americans came back to the United States on a different route. They came home as citizens to a nation that was at last truly free.

Epilogue
The End of Harriet's Journey

ONCE THE WAR ENDED, the soldiers were healed, and all the slaves were freed, Harriet Tubman went home. She moved into the house she'd bought for her parents in Auburn, New York, and cared for them in their old age. In 1869 Harriet married a Civil War veteran. Harriet had met Nelson Davis on a South Carolina army base during the war. Like Harriet, Davis was a former slave. The couple built a house near Harriet's parents' home. They lived there together until Davis died in 1888 after a long struggle with tuberculosis.

Slavery had ended in America. But Harriet Tubman's service to those in need had not. Harriet helped raise money for schools to teach recently freed slaves to read and write. She collected clothes for war orphans and helped the poor, elderly, and disabled. Her efforts eventually led to the building of the Harriet Tubman Home for Aged and Indigent Colored People in Auburn in 1908.

Harriet also worked for women's right to vote, or "suffrage." Harriet Tubman believed that African American equality was linked to equality between men and women. She was a lifelong friend of suffragist pioneer Susan B. Anthony. Both women had been active together in the New England Anti-Slavery Society. When asked whether she thought women should be able to vote, Harriet once said, "I suffered enough to believe it." When Harriet attended the first annual convention of the National Federation of Afro-American Women in 1896 she was given a standing ovation.

While Harriet Tubman received praise and some fame during her lifetime, she was often poor. The proceeds of her first biography, written by neighbor Sarah Bradford in

1868, paid for Harriet's house. But Harriet had to sell vegetables and fruit door-to-door to support her parents and ill husband. She spent the final two years of her life living in the very home for the aged poor that she had helped open. Harriet Tubman died at the age of 93 on March 10, 1913. She was buried with military honors. Her tombstone states, "Servant of God, Well Done."

On the one-year anniversary of her death, a bronze tablet was placed on the courthouse in Auburn, New York. It reads:

HARRIET TUBMAN AT 91 YEARS OF AGE IN 1911.

IN MEMORY OF
HARRIET TUBMAN

Born a slave in Maryland about 1821

Died in Auburn, NY, March 10th, 1913

Called the "Moses" of her people, during the Civil War, with rare courage, she led over three hundred negroes up from slavery to freedom and rendered invaluable service as nurse and spy.

With implicit trust in God she braved every danger and overcame every obstacle, withal she possessed extraordinary foresight and judgment so that she truthfully said—

"On my underground railroad
I nebber run my train off de track
and I nebber los' a passenger."

Glossary

abolitionist a person who believed in ending, or abolishing, slavery

agent Underground Railroad code for a person who plotted a safe course and made arrangements for escaping fugitive slaves

baggage Underground Railroad code for escaping fugitive or runaway slaves

birdshot small lead shot, or bullets, fired from a shotgun

bloodhound a large hound dog with an excellent sense of smell, sometimes used for tracking fugitive slaves

bounty money given as a reward

bounty hunter someone who captures fugitives for the reward money

brakeman Underground Railroad code for a person who helped fugitive slaves find work and homes once in free states or in Canada

buckshot large lead shot, or bullets, fired from a shotgun

cargo Underground Railroad code for fugitive or runaway slaves

chattel personal property that isn't land, including slaves

coffle a chained group of marching prisoners or slaves

conductor Underground Railroad code for a person who guided slaves, or gave directions to slaves on how to escape

Confederacy the Confederate States of America; the 11 southern states that seceded from the United States in 1860 and 1861; also called the Rebel States

contraband goods forbidden by law to be owned or to be brought into or out of a country

contraband slave an enslaved person who escaped to, or was taken behind, Union lines during the Civil War

cotton gin an engine or device for separating seeds from the fiber of a cotton plant

desegregation the end of forced separation of people by their race or religion

drapetomania a made-up disease that people once claimed caused slaves to run away

Drinking Gourd Underground Railroad code for the Big Dipper star grouping, which points to the North Star

driver a slave who supervised other slaves

dysentery a disease of the intestines that produces severe diarrhea

emancipation to be freed from someone else's control or power, especially from slavery

field hand a slave who worked in the fields

flog to beat severely with a rod or whip

forwarding Underground Railroad code for transporting fugitive slaves from station to station

free black a non-enslaved African American during the era of slavery

Free Soiler someone who opposed expanding slavery into the U.S. territories

freedman a person who had been freed from slavery

freedom line Underground Railroad code for the route of travel for an escaped slave

Freedom Train Underground Railroad code for the Underground Railroad

fugitive someone who is fleeing from the law

gorget a crescent-shaped plate hung over the chest, like miniature armor

griot an honored West African storyteller who is also the keeper of the tribe's history

heaven Underground Railroad code for Canada

house slave a slave who worked in the home of a slave owner or master

indentured servant an immigrant contracted to work for an employer for a number of years in exchange for passage on a ship

inferior of little or less importance or value

judgment day Underground Railroad code for time or day of escape

Ku Klux Klan a secret terrorist society, formed after the Civil War, that used violence and murder to promote its white supremacist beliefs

load of potatoes Underground Railroad code for a wagon full of fugitive slaves hidden under farm products, such as hay or potatoes

malaria a disease spread by mosquitoes

marshal a federal law enforcement officer

maroon colonies isolated communities settled by fugitive slaves

master a man who owned slaves

Middle Passage the journey of slave ships from western Africa across the Atlantic to the Americas

mistress a woman who owned slaves

Moses Underground Railroad code for Harriet Tubman

operator Underground Railroad code for an Underground Railroad worker, such as a conductor, an agent, a shepherd, or a stationmaster

overseer an employee of the slave owner who supervised and disciplined slaves

parcel or package Underground Railroad code for arriving fugitive or runaway slaves

passengers Underground Railroad code for escaping fugitive or runaway slaves

plantation a large farm with workers

planter an owner or manager of a plantation

promised land Underground Railroad code for Canada

proslavers people who were in favor of slavery or who supported the institution of slavery

Rebel a person or state in rebellion against the Union during the Civil War; a Confederate

route Underground Railroad code for the course a runaway or group of fugitives took to escape

secede to withdraw from an organization or country

shackle a metal ring or band that prevents free use of the legs or arms

shepherd Underground Railroad code for a person who escorted slaves on their way to freedom

shipment Underground Railroad code for arriving fugitive or runaway slaves

slave a person who is owned by another person and who can be sold at the owner's will

slave auction a place or event where slaves were sold, usually to the highest bidder

slave catcher someone who earned his or her living by finding and capturing runaway slaves for the reward money

slave patroller a person who rode through Southern towns and the Southern countryside looking for runaways

stationmaster Underground Railroad code for a person who ran a safe house

station Underground Railroad code for a safe place where fugitives were sheltered

stockholder Underground Railroad code for someone who donated money, clothing, or food to the Underground Railroad

terminal Underground Railroad code for a town, city, or other such stop on the Underground Railroad

traveler Underground Railroad code for an escaping fugitive or runaway slave

tuberculosis an infectious disease of the lungs

Underground Railroad the secret network of places, people, and pathways that helped slaves escape slavery

Union the United States of America; the Northern states in the Civil War

victuals food

vigilance committee a group who watched for kidnappers and lawmen and protected the free black community

yankee Union soldier or Northerner

Resources

Web Sites to Explore

⊠ National Underground Railroad Network
to Freedom
www.cr.nps.gov/ugrr/
This National Park Service site coordinates
preservation and education efforts associated
with the Underground Railroad all over the
country. There is a lot of general Underground
Railroad information on the site, as well as
shared stories and sites listed by state.

⊠ Aboard the Underground Railroad
www.cr.nps.gov/nr/travel/underground/
ugrrhome.htm
This National Park Service site features the
National Register of Historic Places Travel Itin-
erary, which includes places associated with the
Underground Railroad. The site also includes a

map of the most common directions of escape
taken on the Underground Railroad and other
interesting historic information.

⊠ National Underground Railroad
Freedom Center
www.freedomcenter.org
The Freedom Center is the first national
museum of the Underground Railroad. Its Web
site is a fantastic resource of information and
links about the Underground Railroad. There
are short biographies of abolitionists and
Underground Railroad workers and current
news items, as well as a list of Heritage Sites
listed by state.

Buxton Historic Site & Museum
www.ciaccess.com/~jdnewby/museum.htm
This site tells the story of the Elgin Settlement
of Canada, where many fugitive slaves settled.

National Geographic Interactive Game

www.nationalgeographic.com/features/99/railroad/

This exciting interactive site challenges you to imagine that you are a slave who must decide how to escape. Freedom is only earned after a difficult journey. Are you up for it?

Africans in America: America's Journey Through Slavery

www.pbs.org/wgbh/aia/

The site is the companion to the public television documentary that explores the odyssey of African Africans from the arrival of Europeans in Africa to the Civil War. It is chock-full of information and intriguing original documents.

The William Still Underground Railroad Foundation

www.undergroundrr.com

Readers can find out more about William Still, a leader of the Underground Railroad, at this site.

Exploring the _Amistad_

www.amistadamerica.org

This site recounts the 1839 rebellion aboard the _Amistad_, in which African slaves commandeered the ship, stood trial before the U.S. Supreme Court, and later returned to Africa.

⊠ These sites have Underground Railroad site information and histories organized by state.

Slavery in America

www.slaveryinamerica.org

This educator's site features otherwise hard-to-find resources on the institution of American slavery. It is endorsed by the National Alliance of Black School Educators. It focuses on the experiences of individuals who were enslaved, and it includes narratives, images, and biographies.

Documenting the American South

http://docsouth.unc.edu

This University of North Carolina site includes an amazing collection of Southern history, literature, and culture from the colonial period through the early 1900s. Many of the slave narratives quoted in this book came from works that are also included in this university's online collection. You can read more of the slaves' stories by searching the collection by their names.

American Civil War

www.americancivilwar.com

This site has a large amount of Civil War information about battles, generals, and more. Click on State Battle Maps to see which battles were fought near you. Or find out more about African American soldiers by clicking on Colored Troops.

Books to Read

Bayliss, John F. _Black Slave Narratives._ New York: Macmillan, 1970.

⊠ Bentley, Judith. _Dear Friend: Thomas Garrett & William Still, Collaborators on the Underground Railroad._ New York: Cobblehill, 1997.

⊠ Bentley, Judith. _Harriet Tubman._ New York: Franklin Watts, 1990.

Blassingame, John W. _Slave Testimony: Two Centuries of Letters, Speeches, Interviews, and Autobiographies._ Baton Rouge, LA: Louisiana State University Press, 1977.

⧉ Blockson, Charles L. _The Underground Railroad._ New York: Berkley Publishing Group, 1994.

Bradford, Sarah. _Harriet Tubman: The Moses of Her People._ Bedford, MA: Applewood Books, 1994.

Bradford, Sarah. _Scenes in the Life of Harriet Tubman._ Secaucus, NJ: Citadel, 1961.

Buckmaster, Henrietta. _Let My People Go: The Story of the Underground Railroad and the Growth of the Abolition Movement._ Boston, MA: Beacon Press, 1968.

⊠ Burke, Henry Robert. _The River Jordan: A True Story of the Underground Railroad._ Marietta, OH: Watershed Books, 2001.

Chadwick, Bruce. *Traveling the Underground Railroad: A Visitor's Guide to More than 300 Sites.* Secaucus, NJ: Carol Publishing, 1999.

Conrad, Earl. *General Harriet Tubman.* Washington, DC: Associated Publishers, 1990.

Drew, Benjamin. *A North Side View Slavery.* Westport, CT: Greenwood Publishing Group, 1968.

Fradin, Dennis Brindell. *Bound for the North Star.* New York: Clarion, 2000.

Gates, Henry Louis. *Wonders of the African World.* New York: Knopf, 1999.

Hagedorn, Ann. *Beyond the River: A True Story of the Underground Railroad.* New York: Simon & Schuster, 2003.

Haskins, Jim. *Get On Board: The Story of the Underground Railroad.* New York: Scholastic, 1993.

Hamilton, Virginia. *Many Thousand Gone: African Americans from Slavery to Freedom.* New York: Knopf, 1993.

Katz, William Loren. *Breaking the Chains: African-American Slave Resistance.* New York: Athenaeum, 1990.

Lilley, Stephen R. *Fighters Against American Slavery.* San Diego, CA: Lucent, 1999.

McClard, Megan. *Harriet Tubman: Slavery and the Underground Railroad.* Englewood Cliffs, NJ: Silver Burdett Press, 1991.

Monaghan, Tom. *The Slave Trade.* New York: Raintree Steck-Vaughn, 2003.

Parker, John P. *His Promised Land: The Autobiography of John P. Parker, Former Slave and Conductor on the Underground Railroad.* New York: W. W. Norton & Co., 1996.

Savage, Beth L. *African American Historic Places.* Washington, DC: The Preservation Press, 1994.

Siebert, Wilbur H. *The Underground Railroad from Slavery to Freedom.* New York: Macmillan, 1898.

Still, William. *The Underground Railroad.* New York: Arno Press, 1968.

Taylor, Yuval. *I Was Born a Slave: An Anthology of Classic Slave Narratives.* Chicago, IL: Lawrence Hill, 1999.

These books were written for young readers.

These books have Underground Railroad information and histories organized by state.

Index